The Knowleage

How to be an effective
and emotionally intelligent leader

The Knowledge

How to be an effective and emotionally intelligent leader

Michael Massey

Copyright © 2003 Michael Massey

Apart from any fair dealing for the purposes of research or private study, or criticism or review, as permitted under the Copyright, Designs and Patents Act 1988, this publication may only be reproduced, stored or transmitted, in any form or by any means, with the prior permission in writing of the publishers, or in the case of reprographic reproduction in accordance with the terms of licences issued by the Copyright Licensing Agency. Enquiries concerning reproduction outside those terms should be sent to the publishers.

Troubador Publishing Ltd
12 Manor Walk, Coventry Road
Market Harborough
Leics LE16 9BP, UK
Tel: (+44) 1858 468828
Email: books@troubador.co.uk
Web: www.troubador.co.uk

ISBN 1 904744 03 6

Typeset in 11pt Plantin Light by Troubador Publishing Ltd, Market Harborough, UK
Printed and bound by Cambrian Printers, Wales

t² is an imprint of Troubador Publishing

"We should take care not to make the intellect our god.

It has, of course, powerful muscles, but no personality.

It cannot lead, it can only serve."

Albert Einstein

Introduction

'Every day you will make progress. Every step will be fruitful. Yet there will stretch out before you an ever-lengthening, ever-ascending, ever-improving path. You know you will never get to the end of the journey. But this, so far from being discouraging, only adds to the joy of the climb'
Winston Churchill

Leadership is not only for the few. Anyone who has the ambition to be someone needs to begin to think and act like a leader. Learning to be a leader is an exciting and rewarding journey of self-discovery and self-fulfilment. Some of you will find it easy, others less so. Some of you are going to enjoy the experience, others will not, but unless you try you will never find out. If you succeed – and there's no reason why you shouldn't – you will discover new purpose and real meaning to your life. By picking up this book, you've taken the first step.

Through 'The Knowledge' you will discover how to become an effective leader, and learn to appreciate and understand the qualities of leadership. What you will not find in this book are apocryphal stories or tales of mighty executives and their laudable successes. Neither am I taking you on a journey into a world of fantasy or make believe. Reality is the currency of leadership. Instead I want to offer you the opportunity to use the intelligence that you have and the character that you are to become an effective leader. I want you to acquire the ability to ignite passion and inspiration in those you lead. To do this you will need to understand the importance of being emotionally literate, to be self-aware – *to truly know yourself* – and to be prepared to embrace wholeheartedly the disciplines of self-responsibility.

My purpose is to try and 'unwrap', demystify and explain some of the well-worn words and phrases used in the language of leadership, to clear the muddied waters and to propose a way forward that will inspire you to achieve great things and build your self-confidence in the process. Whether you are already an established leader, just stepped on to the 'fast track', or taking the first steps on the road to becoming an effective leader, I hope 'The Knowledge' will help you to realise your true potential and will become a companion and source of guidance whenever a shadow of self-doubt crosses your path.

Leaders are not pre-ordained. There is no pool of individuals with all the right qualities waiting to save us, to show us the way or solve all our problems. Neither is it a title that bestows power or position. Leadership is something that we have to earn from those whom we lead and is therefore a responsibility that has to be realised and clearly understood. Remember that leaders are made not born. They are created through a process of learning, experience and discovery, of practice and principle. It is this process that I have called 'The Knowledge.' I feel a great deal of sympathy for the aspiring leader wading through endless leadership manuals and attending 'inspirational' leadership courses in an attempt to find the Holy Grail. Reshuffling familiar terms and prescriptions without a real understanding of what they mean is at best confusing and at worst fuels feelings of self-doubt and inadequacy. I want to explore and explain a pathway that will be a foundation and guide for you to be able to realise your ambition to be an effective leader. To do this you will need commitment, resolve and above all else, honesty.

PART ONE

DISCOVERY

1

Self-Awareness

> 'He who knows others is wise; he who knows himself is enlightened'
> **Lao-tzu**

If you aspire to lead you must understand who you are. You must know what 'makes you tick'. To be able to understand others you must first understand yourself. As Socrates counselled, 'Know thyself'. Being *self-aware* is one of the primary responsibilities of being a leader. It is also the keystone of emotional intelligence.

So what is self-awareness? Before answering, consider this: 'People who are truly self-aware are honest *about* themselves *to* themselves, *and* to others'. How honest about yourself are you? Think about that for a minute...now ask yourself how honest you think your answer was? Not sure? Don't worry, it's not an easy question to answer without some considered thought, but it's one that requires some honest answers if you are to understand your level of self-awareness.

Self-awareness has been described as 'being aware of your mood and your thoughts about that mood', and 'an ongoing attention to your inner states'. It's both of these, but put more simply, it is a process of paying proper attention to your inner self.

Life for most of us is busy and complicated. In the competitive world we live in we have to keep our wits about us. We must work hard at what we do if we are to survive and prosper. The strains and vicissitudes of everyday life occupy our time and steal our attention. When we relax we like to be entertained. There's so much going on, so much to think about, and never enough time. As a result life is lived on the surface. Little attention is paid to moods or feelings, or the reasons for them. No time. No reason. We are driven by impulse. We forget to remember. We ignore our feelings and our emotions. Our focus is blurred by endless distractions. Your inner self, the other you – or more accurately the *essential* you – gets ignored, suffocated by the minutiae of daily existence. Only when disaster strikes, or the unexpected causes us to stop and think, do we go in search of our second self. Then we find that years of neglect has severed all communication links with our inner selves - 'the lights are on, but there is nobody in'. No help to be had. No understanding to be found. What to do? How do we interpret these feelings, how do we understand these moods? How do we manage these emotions? How can we avoid being swamped by uncontrolled emotions? How can we deal with them dispassionately and be positive and rational? The answer? It's simple. Make contact with your inner self. Don't be shy, you've met before! Start to pay long-overdue attention to your inner self. Try to develop a stream of conscious thought to increase your awareness of your own thought processes. Practice thoughtful self-reflection. This is the way to build self-awareness. Through practice and self-discipline, you will become aware of your moods and why they came about. By observing yourself you will learn to understand and manage your emotions. Through thoughtful reflection you will understand your moods and your feelings and be sympathetic to the moods and feelings of others. This focused awareness will allow you to achieve greater mental clarity and develop a more positive outlook. You will start to feel more in control of your life.

Self-Reflection

The process of communicating with your inner self, *self-reflection*, is simply a space which you create yourself *for* yourself to provoke self-awareness. It's a means of putting the world around you on hold while you analyse, organise and restructure your thoughts. Learn to use it and you will find that not only will your self-awareness increase, but your self-confidence will improve too. Through self-reflection you will become more aware of your strengths and your weaknesses. Of what motivates you and what drives you. What you believe in and what your true values are. You will be able to understand your dreams without being naïve and your hopes without losing touch with reality. You will be able to tune in to your senses, to your inner self, and to achieve a new level of self-understanding.

For self-reflection to work and for you to gain maximum benefit, you will need to set aside time – uninterrupted time, quiet time – to communicate, to analyse, and to reflect. Often finding time can be difficult, but it's important that you do. When you do take the time to reflect, try to establish a pattern or a routine. After a while you will find that you develop the ability to have an on-going conversation with your inner self. Listen to the voice! Trust the voice! This is one of the most important lessons you will *ever* learn. Soon your self-confidence and your self-awareness will start to improve dramatically. Whatever you do don't lose contact! Remember, throughout history the world's greatest leaders have needed time and space to think and to reflect, and so do you.

How you structure your self-reflection is very much up to you. It works best when you construct your own formula. In due course it can become an automatic process. You may find the mnemonic **VALUE** helpful:

Visualise   Visualise the context of your self-reflection – the place, the people, the situation, the atmosphere, the problem.

Analyse	Analyse the situation, the people. Analyse your feelings, your reactions.
Learn	What lessons are there to be learnt?
Understand	Understand the reality and the meaning of the situation.
Evaluate	Evaluate the results of your reflection. What do they mean? What is your reaction/feeling? Does it influence your thinking? What are the consequences?

As you become more practised in the art of self-reflection, think of some penetrating questions that force you to confront the real issues. For example:

- Why did I do that?
- What really happened?'
- Do I fully understand it?
- What effect did it have on me?
- What does it all mean?

Get to the truth and tax your thinking process. The more you know yourself and the more you are able to learn from your experiences – good *and* bad – the more you will achieve.

Reflect as often as you think necessary. Find a time and place when you can gather your thoughts in peace. I like to scroll through thoughts and ideas before I get out of bed in the morning. I also keep a small notebook handy – it can be very useful, particularly when you're 'in flow' and thoughts and ideas are coming thick and fast.

The process of self-reflection is an *essential* leadership discipline, which will be of enormous help to you in your quest to become truly self-aware. It is the keystone of emotional intelligence. Realise its value, become a regular and proficient practitioner, and it will become a very powerful tool for your self-development.

Self-Awareness Reality Check

To become self-aware it is essential that you carry out an accurate self-assessment. Here is a list of questions which you might find useful. All you need is a blank sheet of paper and to answer the questions honestly.

Part 1   YOU

1. What are you good at?
2. What are you bad at?
3. What are your limitations? Make a list of five.
4. What are your strongest points?
5. What are your weakest points?

    Would your peers agree with you?

    Would your direct reports agree with you?

    If not write down why.

6. What limiting beliefs or behaviours keep recurring in your life?
7. What have you done in your life that makes you most proud?

Part 2   MOTIVATION

1. List five things that really motivate you. Write a short sentence on

each one to explain why.

2. What are your hopes and aspirations in your professional life? Make a list of five.

3. What are your hopes and aspirations in your personal life? List as many as you like.

4. What are your dreams?

5. What is your passion in life?

Part 3   FEELINGS

Describe:

1. What makes you happy?
2. What gives you greatest pleasure?
3. What makes you angry?
4. What do you dislike most?
5. What do you feel guilty about?

How do you physically react to these feelings?

Part 4   VALUES

1. Which of the following qualities do you dislike most? List them in order. Write a single sentence to explain how you feel about each one.

    Betrayal

    Dishonesty

    Jealousy

    Deceit

Selfishness

Greed

Envy

2. Which of the following qualities do you respect most? List them in order. Write a single sentence to explain how you feel about each one.

Honesty

Courage

Kindness

Loyalty

Trust

Truthfulness

Once you have completed your reality check, read through it carefully and thoughtfully. Reflect on what you have written. Take each section separately and make as many changes as you like. Add more questions if you think they would be more appropriate. This simple exercise is to get you to address some basic issues about yourself. It's your first important step to becoming more self-aware and achieving better self-understanding.

Self-awareness is knowing the truth about yourself. It's important also to recognise that you need to own (take responsibility for) that truth to fully understand it. This is a prerequisite to becoming an authentic leader.

Self-Confidence

Leaders are expected to be self-confident, but self-confidence is not pre-ordained. It is a hard-won and fragile commodity. The foundation of self-confidence is self-awareness. The more self-aware you are the greater your self-confidence is likely to be. The greater your self-confidence the more likely it is that you will be an effective leader.

So what are the building blocks of self-confidence? There are three main components:

Competence

Be aware of your abilities. Your self-assessment must be accurate and honest – this is fundamental.

Be conscious of your limitations and always work within your competence boundaries.

Be aware of your emotional strengths and weaknesses.

Knowledge

Know your subject. Know your business. Study and learn – there is no excuse for being ill-informed.

To be really effective, be ahead of the game.

Ask questions, evaluate answers.

Diligence

Make the extra effort, go the extra mile.

Adopt a 'terrier-like' attitude. Be focused and determined. Never let go until you are satisfied that you have done your best.

A competent, knowledgeable and diligent leader will have the ability to fend off infectious doubt. Self-confident leaders have an air of self-assurance: a presence and a self-belief which sets them apart from others. They instil confidence in those they lead. In my experience enlightened leaders understand the dangers of becoming over-confident and are all too aware of the cancer of conceit. Humility and wisdom are the ever-watchful guardians of their self-confidence.

Gut feeling – the educated guess

Self-awareness also means being able to recognise and understand your feelings.

Gut feeling – also called intuition – is one of the most important. So what exactly is it? It's the ability to apply your accumulated experience and wisdom to a particular problem or situation – it's an immediate and well-informed guess, an educated guess if you like. But how does it work, is it real or imagined? It is certainly real and definitely not imagined. This is how it works:

Over time we collect huge amounts of information. We register situations, emotions, reactions. We do this consciously and sub-consciously. We learn by our mistakes. We remember what works and what does not work. We learn to understand cause and effect. Importantly we learn how we make decisions and remember how and why we made them. The brain absorbs all this information and stores it until we face a situation which has similarities that it recognises. When this occurs the brain computes the facts and informs us of its decision through our 'gut'. How?

Our 'emotional brain' uses the circuitry that runs from our limbic centre – the part of the brain which governs our impulses and feelings – to our gut, hence the expression 'gut feeling'. So your 'gut feeling' is a reality after all!

What you now have to do is to recognise your gut feeling, your intuition, and know how to use it. You will find that the more self-aware you are the easier it will be for you to 'plug in' to your emotions and to understand what they're saying to you. Of course gut feelings can be wrong or you may interpret them incorrectly – this may be because your self-awareness levels are not good or you've not had much practice. Whatever the case they shouldn't be taken at face value. You should question, interpret and understand them. If you do you will be able to strengthen your decision-making immeasurably.

Try this exercise

Recall the last time you were aware of your 'gut feeling', your intuition. Now write down what you felt and your reactions as follows:

Did you recognise your 'gut feeling'?

Did you understand it?

Did you believe it?

Did you question it?

Did you interpret it?

Did you follow it?

Was it right?

You might find it useful to follow the following process the next time you have a 'gut feeling' about something:

Recognise

Question

Reflect

Compare

Decide

Use your gut feeling, your intuition, to prompt your thinking. Use it to search for options, to challenge your decisions. As an effective leader, the ability to understand and interpret your gut feelings, to be intuitive, to know what feels right, should become second nature.

2

Self-Image

'Everyone you meet is your mirror'
The Dalai Lama

Self-image is about how you see yourself and learning to see yourself through other people's eyes. How do *you* see yourself? How accurate do you think your self-image is? Is it important? Yes, it is. It's vital. Your image of yourself colours what you do, the way you behave, the way you react, and how effective you are.

Think for a moment about some of the things that have influenced you in your life: your education, people, places, successes, failures. The reality is that there are too many to contemplate, and the way in which they have influenced you is impossible to quantify, but all of them have contributed in varying degrees to the way you perceive yourself. I doubt if you'll ever have paid much attention to the formation of your self-image, or even been conscious of it. Perhaps only when asked directly about it will you have given it any thought, but it is very important that your self-image is accurate, that you perceive it correctly, and that you have some understanding of how it developed.

For example, over time, you may have developed a barrier against uncomfortable truths and created pathways for optimism. Reality may have been masked by habit and lack of attention: self-delusion is the likely result. Self-delusion is something we all practice – to varying degrees – consciously and unconsciously. It is a distortion that inhibits our ability to know our true self-image and to function effectively. This is a very familiar scenario. It's your ego-defence mechanism at work.

So what can you do to discover your true self-image? How do you uncover the truth? How do you unscramble distortions and banish self-delusion? The first thing to do is to increase your self-awareness. The more self-aware you are the more accurate your self-image is likely to be. Next, you should become more aware of your own actions and observe how others react to them. Be sensitive to other people's moods and feelings and try and understand the reasons behind them. Solicit information, ask people for feedback – don't be too proud to ask for negative feedback. Become a skilled questioner: it will help you reveal the reality of your self-image. If possible obtain a 360-degree feedback from sources such as your boss, your peers and your direct reports. This will give you a much wider perspective and be extremely useful to you.

As you become more aware of your self-image and how others see you, you may be pleasantly surprised by what you discover. It may, however, not be what you expected. Whatever the case, as you start to understand your *real* self it will raise many questions in your mind. Do I like my real self? What would I like my *ideal* self to be? To realise what you would like your ideal self to be is to connect with your dreams and recognise your passions. It's a connection all leaders need to make. To do this you need to create a vision for yourself, and the best way of doing this is to ask yourself some searching questions:

What do you like best about yourself?

What do you value most about yourself?

What would you like to change?

What would you like to keep / remain the same?

What would you like to develop most?

What is your greatest ambition?

What is the most important thing in your life?

Who are the most important people in your life?

Where do you see yourself in ten years time?

What would you like your life to look like in ten years ?

What would you like to be doing?

Effective leaders have a clear vision of what they would like their ideal self to be. So should you. Reflect on your answers and you will start to get a better idea of what you would like your 'ideal self' to be. To get more clarity, write down your answers and maybe discuss your ideas with friends. Whatever you do don't water down your vision because of what they might think of you. Listen, but be brave. Be resolute. Uncover your passion. Having a clear idea of what you would like your ideal self to be is an essential focus that will enhance your ability to be a truly authentic leader.

Table 1 is a questionnaire designed to test the accuracy of your self-image. I suggest you complete it yourself before giving it to others to give you feedback. There will be some contradictions in the feedback you receive, but the major indicators should be apparent. This is by no means a definitive list of questions. Add further questions of your own if you think it appropriate. Once you have received your feedback compare it to your own – the results could be interesting!

Use the information to guide your efforts in trying to achieve your 'ideal self'. If there are areas that concern you, examine them carefully and work out how you could make improvements.

Table 1 Percentage accuracy – tick the appropriate box

	0-20	20-40	40-60	60-80	80-100
I come across as a positive person					
I am approachable					
I always look on the bright side					
I come across as a happy person					
I am an optimist					
I am intimidating					
I always have time for others					
I am a good communicator					
Nothing is ever too much trouble					
People like my company					
I have a sense of humour					
I am loyal					
I don't gossip					
I am trustworthy					
I am regarded as a hard worker					
I have sound judgement					
People can confide in me					
I make sound decisions					

Self-Image

	0-20	20-40	40-60	60-80	80-100
I am a good listener					
I delegate					
I conduct meetings well					
I am tolerant					
I motivate others					
I communicate my vision					
I instil confidence					
I confront issues					
I am pro-active rather than re-active					
People believe I care about them					
I support my staff					
I am self-confident					
I deal with conflict issues well					
I am regarded as ambitious					
I am an inspirational leader					
I am helpful in a crisis					
I keep calm					
I help others develop					

The Knowledge

	0-20	20-40	40-60	60-80	80-100
I learn from my mistakes					
I don't blame others					
I praise good work					
My criticism is always constructive					
I don't bear grudges					
I am creative					
I don't avoid issues					
I am not afraid to ask for help					
I plan and prepare well					
I am a good questioner					
I empathise					
I always try to see the other viewpoint					

3
Self-Management

'We are being judged by a new yardstick: not just how smart we are, or by our training and expertise, but also by how we handle ourselves and each other'
Daniel Goleman

I am amazed at the number of people who raise a questioning eyebrow when I talk about 'self-management.' 'What makes you think I need to manage myself?' is the unasked question. The way we go about our daily lives is something we do subconsciously. It's not something we actually have to think about, far less discuss. The truth is that most people pay little attention to managing their lives. Habit, routine and circumstance have become our masters, and give us the comforting impression that there is some kind of order in our lives when in fact there is very little. We are happy to deal with events as they happen, and only when an event occurs which prompts us to take stock do we express surprise at the way events have unfolded or a relationship has turned out. This is not the way an effective leader can afford to operate.

Self-management is the hallmark of responsible leadership.

How good you are at it will depend on whether you make the right choices, take the right decisions and whether you act on them. Being an effective self-manager means that you have the will and the self-discipline to make it work. It's also about putting first things first and having the will to do things you don't like doing when they need to be done. So where to begin? Effective self-management requires self-confidence, which is derived from self-knowledge. As a first step, therefore, I think the best thing would be to establish a base line to help you find focus before examining what I call the 'personal' aspects of self-management. You may also find it useful to use the headings as prompts in periods of self-reflection – as part of a self-auditing process if you like.

To start you off, I've listed a number of questions I would like you to ask yourself. No doubt you will have others you will want to add, but this will be a useful start. It will enable you to get these important aspects of your life into better perspective, help you to be clear about how successful you've been at self-management so far, and give you an indication of what you've got to do!

Direction	Do you have a clear direction in your life? Have you set yourself goals and if so, are they realistic and achievable? Are you happy with this direction? If not, what would you change?
Conduct	What influences and controls the conduct of your life? Is your life ruled by routine and habit? Does it have any structure? If you wanted to, what could you do to effect change?
Purpose	Do you have a clear sense of purpose? What is it?
Influence	What are the major influences in your life? How important are they to you? Do you consider them all positive influences or are there some negative ones you would rather do without? If so, how would you go about removing them?

Vision Do you have a clear vision of what you want to achieve in your working life? Is this a fixed vision or do you revise it from time to time? How does your vision fit into your private life?

Responsibility Does responsibility sit easily on your shoulders? Do you understand what your responsibilities are and what they mean?

Work/Life Balance Do you have one and if so are you comfortable with it? Are you prepared to make sacrifices in order to achieve your goals? Do you weigh this against the effect this might have on the balance of your life?

Reflect on your answers.

Behaviour

There are two aspects of self-management that require special attention. The first is how you conduct yourself, in other words your behaviour. The second is how you manage your emotions. As a leader you are constantly under scrutiny. Your every move is noted: what you do, what you say, how you say it and how you react. Those whom you lead are always aware of your mood. They learn to recognise your body language, they are keenly aware of your behaviour; many try to read your thoughts and follow your example. It is therefore crucially important that you are aware of your feelings and the way they affect your actions. The next time you hold a meeting with your staff, watch their reactions as they come into the room. One of the first things they will do is to look at you and try and pick up what sort of mood you are in. If you are careless and allow your behaviour to betray your feelings – whatever they may be – you will severely limit your options and possibly affect the outcome of the meeting.

Managing your Emotions

Containing and managing your emotions intelligently is the mark of a well-adjusted and effective leader. One attribute which makes this process considerably easier – and one you need to develop – is sensitivity. If you are sensitive to situations and atmospheres, sensitive to people, to the way they feel, sensitive to the effects of what you say and the decisions you take, you will have found a very positive way of educating your feelings and, thereby, a means of managing your emotions effectively and responsibly.

Remember that emotions are infectious. They are picked up on very quickly. This is a positive advantage when it comes to emotions like enthusiasm and optimism, but it is a very different story when it comes to negative emotions such as anger, frustration and anxiety.

The management and control of the feelings that spark negative emotions is an essential piece of equipment in a leader's toolbox. To be able to 'keep your head while those around you are losing theirs' – and to remain positive and optimistic when things are really tough – is what will mark you out as a leader and inspire others to want to support you and to follow you.

No doubt you have been under enormous pressure many times and have been involved in a major crisis more times than perhaps you care to remember. Can you recall the overwhelming feeling you experienced at the time: panic, extreme anxiety, fear, perhaps all three? I expect you found it extremely difficult to think straight and focus on what needed to be done. Am I right? You'd be pretty unusual if you didn't. It's at times like these that intelligent leaders call on an essential resource which comes from the important skill and discipline of self-management. This is the ability to manage your feelings, and to bypass the disruptive, negative emotions that cloud and confuse clear and level-headed thinking. You need to be able to rise above the emotional interferences activated by out-of-control feelings. Learning to manage your feelings will enable you to be positive and to generate optimism that will significantly enhance your standing as a leader. Respect and trust from your followers will be your reward.

Whatever you do remember that emotions are infectious. If you allow yourself to display a feeling of, say, anger or frustration, it will be picked up immediately, and thereafter will colour the tone and perhaps even the outcome of the conversation. It is a luxury you cannot afford. Equally, you need to be aware of how you react to emotions expressed by others. If you use your self-management skills to carefully weigh your reaction to the emotion being expressed, you will find yourself in a far stronger position to make sense of complicated problems, avoid confrontation and produce a positive outcome.

Managing Moods

In the general scheme of things, moods may seem to be relatively unimportant. Compared to emotions, which can be powerful and have a dramatic effect, moods are milder and tend to linger rather than invade. The effect of a negative or bad mood, however, should not be underestimated. It is highly infectious, and can have a deeply corrosive effect on attitudes if it is allowed to spread.

People are extremely sensitive to the moods of their leaders, so it is very important that you develop the ability to recognise and identify your mood. How do moods develop? Let's take a very simple example.

EXAMPLE

You shut your front door a little more firmly than usual leaving behind a smouldering domestic issue. It's raining. Your train is late. It's crowded. When you arrive at the office you discover that a vital document you need for a meeting has not arrived. Understandably you are angry, frustrated and anxious: not a good way to start the day. You have an important meeting scheduled for ten o'clock. It is a particularly sensitive meeting and you need it to go well. So what about your mood?

Not good? Carry it into that meeting and you will infect everyone else and seriously jeopardise the outcome. In circumstances like these you have to recognise your mood and leave it outside the door of the meeting room. Easier said than done? Possibly, but you must do it. The key lies in your ability to be aware of your mood in the first place and then to know how to do something about it.

> **Be aware of your mood**
>
> **Check your mood**
>
> **Change your mood**

To change your mood you need to be aware of it. Depending on what sort of mood it is it may simply be a question of self-discipline. You may however have to employ a degree of stagecraft. Humour is sometimes a useful catalyst for mood change although it is not always appropriate.

Just consider for a moment how many meetings you have taken or attended that might have been affected by your mood? The outcome of a meeting can so easily be affected by an uncontrolled or unrecognised mood. To allow this to happen is selfish and irresponsible. It is very important to remember that as a leader, it is your responsibility not to infect others with your bad mood, no matter how difficult it may be.

The good mood virus is a different matter. This is something you hope everybody catches. It's amazing how everything gets done when everyone is in a good mood. There's a feeling of optimism, people are helpful and considerate, and somehow problems seem to evaporate. As corrosive as a bad mood can be, so good moods produce harmony, inspire performance and act as a positive tonic. Good moods are not conjured out of thin air, but they can be promoted by humour and a positive attitude. This is the job of the leader. Leaders need to be particularly sensitive to their own moods and the moods of others, and be able to move them towards the positive. The benefits of doing so are enormous both in terms of individual performance and bottom-line results. It's simple. Good moods are good for business. Bad moods are bad for business.

Climate Control

It is remarkable the amount of time it takes for some leaders to realise – if they ever do – how much their moods can affect the climate of an organisation. There is a clear and direct link between the quality of the human climate and performance. Unfortunately, the link is often not made and frequently ignored. Ineffective and insensitive leadership, coupled with a lack of self-awareness, is usually to blame. It is frightening to think how much one person's selfishness can affect the performance of an organisation and the lives of others. The ability of a leader to be able to manage his moods can be the difference between success and failure. All it really takes is a little extra effort, a little extra thought. Take the temperature in your organisation and be aware of your effect on it. Learn to be sensitive to climate. Learn to be sensitive to atmospheres. Learn to manage your moods. Climate control is a fundamental element of self-management which no leader can afford to ignore.

Time

The notice on the Chief Executive's desk read 'Beware of Thieves'. This didn't mean that his office furniture was about to be removed or that there were pickpockets about. This was a reminder that the greatest threat to his ability to act efficiently was the theft of time. All organisations are filled with time thieves. The over-zealous secretary, the chatty colleague, the interfering boss, the persistent caller: they are all time thieves. They prey on the disorganised, the careless and the ill-prepared. Their effect can be devastating, causing deadlines to be missed, appointments to be delayed and a lot of unnecessary pressure. Their effect on your personal life can be serious too. You'll be the one in your office dealing with the after-effects of their actions, burning the midnight oil when the thieves are sitting comfortably at home believing they've done a good day's work.

Crime prevention is the duty of every leader! The best way of preventing time theft is not by managing *time*, but by managing *yourself*. Always having a weekly schedule, a monthly plan and possibly a six-month overview with clearly-defined goals, *and* by having the will and the self-discipline to keep to them, will go a long way to eliminating this heinous crime. Organising and prioritising within your weekly schedule will also act as a deterrent, but be careful not to make a straightjacket for yourself. You need some freedom and flexibility to maintain spontaneity and to grasp opportunity when it arises.

Time Check

Attack the crime, but more importantly attack the causes of the crime! You might find it useful to work through a typical day or week and see if you can identify whether there has been any time crime committed and whether your crime prevention methods need improving.

Access	Does everyone have access to you at any time? How much time do you estimate you spend with unscheduled callers? Can you identify individuals who absorb your time unnecessarily?
Telephone management:	Do you manage your telephone calls efficiently? Do you screen or filter your calls? Do you leave your mobile on when you're in the office? What do you do about personal calls?

e-mails	How much time do you devote to reading your e-mails? Do you deal with e-mails as they arrive or do you set aside time to do that?
Meetings	Do you chair meetings effectively? Do your meetings start when they are scheduled to start? Do you allow meetings to over-run? Do you allow others to hijack your day with unscheduled meetings or 'quick chats'?
Staff	Are your staffing levels correct? Have you got sufficient support to allow you to do your job well? When things are tight do you have reliable and competent staff you can delegate to?
Personal	Do you allow your day-to-day personal life to interfere with your business life? How good is your timekeeping?
Schedule revision	Do you review and consider your weekly schedule on a daily basis? Do you review your monthly schedule at least once a week? How often do you review your long-term plans?

Examine your routine. Eliminate bad habits. Always be aware of how your time is spent. It's very valuable. Spend it wisely. Adopt your own crime prevention policy. Put an end to time crime. Manage yourself and you will manage your time.

4

Self-Development

> *'Learning is a discovery, but learning doesn't happen unless you're looking'*
> **John Dewey**

The days have long since passed when, in exchange for your loyalty and hard work, you could expect an implied promise of security and a career path. Today the only security you have is determined by the standard of your performance. The comforting cloak of company identity is threadbare, and the reassuring but probably illusory feeling that someone is looking after your interests has disappeared. The bottom line is that organisations no longer want the responsibility of looking after people – certainly not in the way they used to in the past. Individuals – and leaders in particular – are very much on their own. 'Looking after number one' has taken on a new meaning. The emphasis now is on individuals taking responsibility for their own development. This new environment means that leaders have a special responsibility for their own self-development, because of the important role they play in people's lives.

So what is self-development? Self-development is primarily about learning. Learning should always be part of your agenda. It is such a vital ingredient in the process of your development as an effective leader. By learning I don't mean simply the acquisition of more knowledge, or knowing all the answers. In the context of leadership, it's about growth and understanding. It's true to say that those leaders who have a clear idea of who they are and where they want to be, and take responsibility for themselves, find learning easy and rewarding. As John Dewey remarked, 'learning is discovery'. Someone else said that 'curiosity is the mother of discovery.' Curiosity is the sign of an active mind, and is a most important leadership quality.

Your Learning Plan

I don't believe that meaningful self-development can take place unless it is formalised in some way. Unless it is, the pressures of daily life are such that it will simply become another good intention that never gets realised. A 'learning plan' is what is required. I'm aware that much of your time may already be taken up planning, so please don't be put off by this. What I'm proposing is a learning plan which will help you map out where you want to be and will enable you to set yourself clear personal learning goals. These learning goals should reflect your aims and aspirations, and motivate you to improve and grow as a leader. Don't confuse performance goals with learning goals. Learning goals are *not* measures of performance or success.

The most successful learning plans are the ones that leaders create for themselves. A good plan will have 'what you want to become' as its main focus. It should be about improvement rather than performance. It should highlight your talents and motivate you to want to learn. If you really believe in your plan and want to make it work you will be surprised by the results and how quickly you learn. I guarantee that you'll find it a very rewarding experience.

A successful plan must have realistic and well-thought-through goals. Goals are essential because they create focus. They are the most effective way of achieving positive results, but choose your goals carefully. They should be *your* goals and not those imposed by others or influenced by comments in your latest assessment. You need to own your goals for them to work. Don't forget this plan is about *your* development and what *you* want to become. Set aside time to think about them carefully. I would recommend that initially you focus on two or three at the most. Base all your goals on your strengths, not your weaknesses. Remember, this is not a remedial process: it's a growing process and one which is aimed at assisting you in achieving your aims and ambitions. Your learning plan will help you set your course for the future.

There is no right or wrong way to produce a learning plan. It's very much a personal thing, so spend some time considering how you would like your plan to look. Set it out and see what it looks like. Why not start by asking yourself two fundamental questions:

What do I really want to learn?

What would be of greatest benefit for me to learn?

What you might want to learn may not be of greatest benefit to you and vice versa. It might be a good idea to make a list under each heading and then prioritise them – regardless of category. This should make the choice of which learning goals to pursue a little easier.

What's the best way to learn? You will have your preferences, I'm sure. Choose the one that you are most comfortable with and which best suits the topic. It should be the one which you believe will benefit your learning most. For instance, you may decide that the best way for you to learn would be to do a detailed study. Your learning could be experiential. You could learn from example or through practice. You could experiment and use trial and error to achieve your goal or a combination of any of these. It's up to you.

Don't be over-ambitious in setting your learning goals. Remember that you have to find time to learn. Whatever you do don't let your plan interfere with your work or dislocate your family life. If you do you will start to resent your plan and it will wither and die. Make space for your learning. Be purposeful and resolute. The dividends will surprise you.

Before committing yourself to your learning plan, ask yourself the following questions about the goals you have set yourself:

Are the goals I have set realistic?

Are they focused on my strengths?

Do I believe in them?

Do they cover things that I need to learn to develop as a leader?

Do they form part of my overall vision?

How will I measure success?

When do I want to achieve these goals?

Like all plans, yours will need to be updated as you work through your goals. Frequent revision is a good thing. If one of your goals isn't working don't worry about it! Either revise it or drop it, but don't let it bring down the rest of your plan.

If you have doubts about your whole plan, make a new one. Take some time out to reflect and set yourself new goals. Whatever you do make sure your goals are realistic and achievable. If they're not, the plan will fail. Be confident that you will eventually come up with a plan that you are happy with – one which will produce the results you are looking for.

Reflective Visioning

This is a practice that I find very useful and one which I think would be very helpful to you when you start to produce your learning plan. I believe that it will help you to establish the right goals. I call it reflective visioning. This is simply a mental visioning exercise which allows you to achieve focus – to rehearse the future. If you can *visualise* a situation it will be easier to understand. If you *imagine* an event or a way of approaching a problem it will seem clearer and easier to deal with should it occur. The process will raise questions and uncover doubts which you can address *in advance*. Let's look at reflective visioning more closely, because it's such a useful thing to be able to do. This example might make it easier to understand.

EXAMPLE

You have to make a presentation to the board at the end of the week about the restructuring of your division. You're nervous about the proposals you're going to make, not only because they're far-reaching, but also because your predecessor now sits on the board, and your proposals effectively dismantle everything he put in place when he had your job. You're worried about the questions you will be asked and whether you can put your case across convincingly.

For the three days leading up to the meeting you take time out to go through the questions you might be asked. You rehearse your answers. You picture yourself in the boardroom making your presentation and go over the main points of your presentation. You anticipate the negative reaction from your predecessor and visualise the scene and your reaction. You maintain your focus and envisage yourself achieving a positive outcome. When you come to present your case you feel at ease. You put your case clearly and answer the questions positively. Your predecessor accepts your well-reasoned arguments and your proposals are accepted.

Reflective visioning should be an integral part of a leader's thinking process. Anticipating events and their consequences helps leaders be one step ahead and to always appear to have the right answer. It is a highly creative mechanism which provokes new and original thought. It's also the reason why many leaders find it difficult to 'switch off' because it stimulates so many interesting and exciting thoughts and ideas. It is something that, as a leader, you should practice and learn to use. All it requires is the will to start and the mental discipline to be able to use it effectively.

Reflective visioning produces amazing mental clarity. So why not apply reflective visioning to the production of your learning plan? *Visualise* what you want to become, for example. *Imagine* the changes that might occur if you achieved your learning goals and how this might enhance your performance. I guarantee you'll find it a very worthwhile exercise. It will help give your plan clarity and purpose and make your goals clearer. It is a very powerful tool.

Reframing

An important part of the process of learning is to be able to reframe your thinking. To be able to view situations, problems – people even – in a way that stimulates creative and constructive thought. Reframing is about looking at things from a different perspective, about taking a problem and turning it inside out. It's looking at it from the other person's point of view, it's imagining a totally different context. Above all, it's about regarding something as an opportunity rather than a problem. Reframing makes problems easier to understand and therefore easier to solve.

Successful businesses are constantly reframing. So should you. Reframe your talents, your strengths *and* your weaknesses. Recognise when it would be wise to re-deploy your efforts so that they can be more effective. Reframe your mindset to 'opportunity mode'. This is territory where you might find it an advantage to have the help of a navigator, i.e. a coach. (I will have more to say about coaches and coaching later.)

Leaders need to be creative in thought and deed. Reframing is an amazing means of stimulating creativity. It is a very exciting and rewarding process. It unlocks the shackles of one-dimensional thinking and sparks new thought. Practise it until it becomes a habit. It will greatly enhance your effectiveness as a leader.

5

Self-Responsibility

'I don't know the key to success, but the key to failure is trying to please everybody'
Bill Cosby

As a leader, your natural instincts are to put the interests of others ahead of your own. You are responsible for those you lead – they are, after all, your most valuable assets – so it is a perfectly proper and laudable thing for you to do, but you have a responsibility to yourself too. If you are tired, stressed out and your life is in chaos, your effectiveness will be seriously compromised. The decisions you take will be ill-considered and probably wrong, and your working relationships will start to disintegrate. You will almost certainly start to 'lose the plot', and any respect that you might have gained from those you lead will start to evaporate. You will have started on the downward spiral that eventually leads to the door marked 'Exit'.

It is totally irresponsible for any leader not to understand the importance of self-responsibility.

What do I mean by self-responsibility? Self-responsibility

is the care and attention you pay to yourself. The way you plan, conduct and organise your life, at home and at work; the way you organise your time, the attention you pay to your health and well-being. All these things affect your ability to function as an effective leader. You need to practise what I call 'responsible selfishness'. I hope this label sticks in your memory because your own well-being should always be at the forefront of your mind – not only for your own benefit but also for the benefit of those you lead. They will be first to suffer the consequences if you become neglectful!

When there's a crisis in the office it's very easy to start to ignore even the basic things in life like eating properly, getting enough sleep, taking exercise, spending time with your friends and family. Often you become so totally immersed in a project that it takes over your life. As a responsible leader you will have to work as hard at prioritising and organising your own life as you do others' – probably harder – if you are to stay mentally and physically ahead of the game. It is not a question of 'finding time' to do this, but *organising* time and planning ahead. After that it's having the self-discipline to make sure you keep to your plan. If you don't, the chances are that events will start to control your life and you will lose all sense of direction and perspective. Problems multiply at work and at home, and any creative energy that you might have had is taken up fire-fighting the results of your neglect.

Stress

Many might argue that if you're a leader, stress comes with the territory. It is true that leadership can be stressful and it's not difficult to imagine why. Leaders are always under the spotlight: their actions are constantly under scrutiny and their motives ruthlessly judged. They often feel alone, anxious, and under pressure – a perfect recipe for stress. It is therefore imperative that you understand what happens when you become stressed, how to recognise it, and how to deal with it.

When you become stressed your brain is programmed to react to what it perceives as 'the threat' by allowing stress hormones to be secreted. These hormones raise your blood pressure and prepare you for action. One of these hormones, cortisol – which is longer-lasting than the others – has the effect of inhibiting your learning processes so that you concentrate on using your instinctive habits to defend yourself. If the stress does not stop, cortisol will go on being secreted and will continue to affect your learning process. Research shows that sustained stress and excretion of cortisol actually *kills off* the brain cells needed for new learning. If you remember that 'stress makes you stupid!' it should prompt you to respect the effect that stress can have.

Stress cannot be avoided, but it is imperative that you manage it successfully because it affects the way you react and inhibits learning. So what is the best way of handling stress?

Exercise! Regular exercise, preferably aerobic, can reduce stress levels significantly. Exercise is also a potent anti-depressant. Not got the time? Make time.

Meditation. Stop and take time out to pay attention to what is happening in the moment. This is a very beneficial way of clearing down confused thoughts and frustrations. Meditation may not be 'your thing', but if you think that it might be, learn how to do it properly.

Moderate alcohol intake. Alcohol actually sensitises the stress response and makes it more effective. So when you're stressed it really doesn't pay to reach for the bottle – it'll just make things worse. Alcohol is also the cause of the alarm bell that wakes you at 3 am for a meeting you'd rather not have. When you're under stress the rule is: less not more.

Take a break! Some people become so stressed that they consider taking a break is a dereliction of duty. You see it really can make you stupid! It is vital that you take breaks during the day and that you plan and organise your holidays. Re-charging your batteries is vital if you are going to function effectively.

Learn your stress signals. Learn what your reactions to stress are. Irritability, sleepless nights, intolerance, abruptness – whatever they are, recognise them and do something about it when they occur.

Create structure. Stress can easily occur when there is no order in your life, when events are controlling you. Plan and think ahead.

Prepare for the unexpected. Reflective visioning, which I mentioned earlier, is a powerful means of containing stress. Your ability to envisage a problem or situation and then consider your reaction to it will significantly reduce your stress levels.

Dealing with your own stress is one thing, but do you create stress in others? If you do, you need to ask yourself why and do something about it. Leaders are not meant to pass on stress. They should be able to contain it and stop it from infecting those they lead. Whatever your style of leadership, communicating your own stress or exerting pressure in a careless and unintelligent manner likely to cause stress in others is irresponsible and counterproductive. It is also seriously de-motivating and is definitely not the mark of a good leader.

A final word about stress. Stress can be extremely harmful. Manage your stress – well. Know your limits. Know the signs. Be a friend to yourself and be selfish about stress.

Health

In the same way that you might be justified in questioning the judgement of a doctor who smoked, a leader who failed to look after his health might justifiably attract the same questions. This might sound a little harsh, but if you ignore your physical health, your mental health will soon suffer and your ability to perform effectively will be severely curtailed. Today, athletes and sportsmen and women spend as much time exercising and training their minds as they do their bodies. They realise that to achieve optimum performance they need to be both mentally and physically fit. Just like an athlete, a responsible leader is constantly under pressure to perform well. Mentally you may be gold medal standard, but if you're unfit and ignore your physical well-being, your performance will suffer. Like the athlete, you need to be physically *and* mentally fit to perform to your best ability. Many people argue that the pressures of work and family life make it difficult to find time to take regular exercise. I don't buy that argument. The more often you take physical exercise the better you will feel and the harder you'll try to find time.

'You are what you eat'. I'm sure you've heard that statement before. The pressure of the busy working day can easily have an adverse effect on your eating habits. An insufficient breakfast followed by high sugar content snacks and too much caffeine can turn you into a mad bull or a raging virago by lunchtime and a bear with a sore head by four o'clock. If you are going to perform at your best you need to pay attention to what you eat, not just during the day, but to your whole diet. To an intelligent leader this is not too much to ask. It may seem unimportant in the scheme of things, but your diet is actually very important indeed and needs to be organised, like everything else.

Successful leaders must be ahead of the game. There is one sure way to lose your edge and that is to deprive yourself of adequate sleep. Fatigue stupefies. It dulls your senses, slows your reactions, shortens your temper and skews your emotional balance. It affects your judgement. It destroys optimism and suffocates good humour. It is the enemy of effective leadership.

There is nothing heroic about staying late or being the last to leave the office. It's not a sign of fortitude. It's a sign of weakness and personal indiscipline. It's also unintelligent. I would strongly recommend that you examine your attitude to sleep. Ask yourself:

Do you regard your ability to 'keep going' at all costs as a strength?

Do you ever think about how much sleep you need?

Do you recognise signs of fatigue?

Do you ever do anything about it?

Become aware of the benefits of adequate sleep and you could improve the quality of your life immeasurably – you'll be more effective too. All it takes is a little self-discipline.

Think of your body as a machine. Look after it and it will not let you down. Abuse it and it will break down. Breakdowns happen at inconvenient times and when you're least expecting them. It would be unfortunate if, through neglect, a breakdown occurred just as you were about to realise your lifelong goal. As a responsible leader, it is important that you understand that the benefits of physical exercise and keeping yourself healthy are enormous.

6

Relationship Management

'You can make more friends in two months by becoming interested in other people than you can in two years by trying to get other people interested in you'
Dale Carnegie

In a climate where command and control have been superseded by persuasion and collaboration, the need to be able to manage relationships skilfully has become one of the most important leadership qualities. It is a highly prized expertise. Today, leaders are as likely to be judged on the strength of their ability to manage interpersonal relationships as anything else. To do this effectively they need to be aware of their emotions, to understand their values and their visions before they can have any chance of being able to understand others.

Relationship management is a very special skill. It is not something that just 'happens'. You don't succeed just because you're nice to know or you have a friendly face. It requires alertness, attention and sensitivity. Alertness to people's behaviour: you read them well, you notice change and you notice attitude. You pay attention to what they say, to what they *don't* say, and to their body language. You are sensitive to their emotions and their feelings. Gradually you are able to 'get onto their wavelength' and make a connection, you build a rapport. Your actions confirm your conviction and the honesty of your purpose. This is what is called empathy. Through empathy your leadership develops authenticity, and authenticity is a leadership passkey. It opens essential doors which make effective leadership possible.

Empathy

Empathy's foundation is self-awareness. It's about being socially aware too. Empathy is about consideration: the consideration of others, understanding their perspectives and their feelings, their emotions, their hopes and aspirations. It's about creating harmony. It's about understanding other people's points of view. It's about listening carefully to what people have to say, and about responding intelligently and sensitively. Empathy is a very important dimension of emotional intelligence. To perfect it takes practice and a lot of self-discipline. Of the essential skills required to be able to empathise, *listening to understand* and *being able to question effectively and sensitively* are probably the most important. Once your listening skills improve, you will find that you start to 'notice' so much more of what is being said and what is not said. You'll consider other people's points of view more, you'll notice their non-verbal language such as body language, and you'll become far more aware of their attitudes and how they react. Consequently your responses are likely to be more thoughtful and considered, which will allow that essential connection to be made. With practice you will find that you become more interested, more attentive and more able to recognise the needs and understand the feelings of others.

For leaders to be effective they need to 'tune in' to those they lead. They have to understand them. They have to know how they feel, understand their emotions. When there is that understanding and the connection has been made, it opens up amazing opportunities for a leader to react appropriately. On one level, sharing visions and values and on another sharing highs and lows. It allows a clearer insight into the emotional reality of an individual or a group. With this level of understanding there is less *mis*understanding. It is easier to get the message across with conviction and with authenticity. Decisions are better informed and performance benefits as a result.

The trust and confidence that empathy can engender offer leaders the opportunity to use the connection that has been built up to generate positive emotions, to promote optimism, to focus aspirations and ambitions, to motivate and to inspire. If you think of some of the world's greatest leaders, the one thing they have in common is that they all made a connection with their audience. They understood people's feelings and emotions and the people recognised this.

In today's environment the emotional illiterate is a hindrance and probably a liability too. The disharmony and disruption they can cause is extremely damaging, no matter how good they might be at their job. Like the boor and the bully, their inability to show empathy casts considerable doubt on their judgement. This shortcoming devalues their ability to make a selfless and positive contribution.

Of all the diseases which can exist within an organisation, there is one which causes untold harm and disruption, but is seldom recognised. It is the cancer of doubt. Doubt lingers in the back of people's minds. Left untreated it mutates into fear, which causes paralysis. The most effective cure for this terrible disease is empathy. The skill of an attentive and emotionally intelligent leader who makes that essential connection with the patient can cause an almost instantaneous cure. If the attention continues the disease is unlikely to reappear and the individual's performance improves dramatically.

Empathy is a critical skill which is essential not only in our business lives, but in our personal lives too.

7

Coaching

'I never cease to be amazed at the power of the coaching process to draw out the skills or talent that was previously hidden within an individual, and which invariably finds a way to solve a problem previously thought unsolvable'
**John Russell, Managing Director,
Harley-Davidson Europe Ltd.**

It's lonely at the top. When you become a leader, one of the drawbacks of your success may be that you lose the freedom to discuss things as openly with your boss or your peers as you did in the past. It is naïve and unrealistic to think that you could, particularly in a competitive environment. Nevertheless, your need for someone to talk to, for someone to assist you in your development as a leader – someone who will help you realise your full potential – has not diminished. It has increased. Remember, if you want to achieve your ambitions you have to take responsibility for your own leadership development. If you are to survive in this new, lonely and challenging environment you have to do some thing about it. Enter the coach.

What exactly is coaching ? Tim Gallwey, a Harvard educationalist and tennis expert, describes it as follows:

'Coaching is unlocking a person's potential to maximise their own performance. It is helping them to learn rather than teaching them.'

Coaching is a process of facilitating performance, learning, and development through one-to-one dialogue. It raises awareness and responsibility through open and effective questioning, and creates an environment where individual learning and reflection can take place. It helps you develop self-awareness and mental clarity. It's about developing from within.

So why should you employ a coach? Well, if you want to raise and sustain your game and reach your true potential – if you want to truly develop as a leader – I would strongly recommend that you employ a coach. A coach can be an objective, confidential sounding board to test your thinking – someone to talk to in periods of pressure and stress. A coach can be another voice with a totally independent viewpoint to help you see over the wall that surrounds your life. Coaching offers you a unique opportunity to create space, space for you to reflect on important issues, to consider alternatives and new perspectives, and to develop your leadership strengths. It is a powerful learning experience. My recommendation would be that you arrange to have a trial coaching session. Selecting the right coach is very important. You should look for an executive coach whom you feel has the right background and experience. Here are some tips:

Ask for an initial meeting and then afterwards ask yourself the following questions:

1. Do you like the person – is the 'chemistry' right?
2. Did they talk a lot? (bad sign)

3. Did they listen well? (good sign)
4. Would you look forward to spending time in their company?
5. Were you interested / stimulated by the experience?
6. Did they show interest in you and your situation?
7. Did they show energy and enthusiasm?
8. Do you think they could help you develop as a leader?
9. Ask them how they would work with you – are you happy with their answer?
10. Ask them about their background, experience and training.

If you are satisfied with your answers and you think that you could get on with your coach, then arrange a time and place to meet again. The second meeting usually takes the form of a 'diagnostic review', which will cover things like your current situation, your career to date, your personal values, attitudes and beliefs, your family background, your skills, and your aspirations and ambitions. During this meeting your coach should be establishing a working relationship with you and building a clear picture of you. A good coach will want to know your personal strengths. He will want to understand your organisation, its culture and the role you play in it, so that an appropriate agenda can be agreed and goals defined. You should set your goals with your coach. These are likely to be a mixture of professional and personal goals. Finally, you need to agree the coaching programme. The frequency of your sessions is entirely up to you, but typically will be a one-and-a-half hour session every 2–3 weeks for the first three months and thereafter monthly for as long as required. A typical contract is likely to be for nine months, but can be significantly longer. The choice is yours. Your coach is likely to use one of several coaching models during your coaching sessions. I have outlined one of these – the INTO GROW model – in Appendix A. This will give you an idea of what to expect. Most coaches do not adhere rigidly to a coaching model, but use one such as the INTO GROW model as a framework for the coaching style they have developed for themselves.

If you find that you get on with your coach and you're deriving real benefit from your coaching sessions, you have several options open to you. You can extend your contract for whatever period you like or enter into a new contract with a new agenda and new goals. You can decide not renew the contract and come back to coaching at a later date – either with your current coach or a new one – or amend the frequency of your sessions. There is a lot of merit in having the support of your coach as a sounding board after your coaching contract has ended – to keep them on a retainer – particularly if you have found a good one. There will be times when you need that sounding board and when you will need coaching.

Coaching can provide invaluable support and greatly assist your development as a leader. With a good coach it no longer has to be lonely at the top.

8

Attitude

'Attitude is a little thing that makes a big difference'
Winston Churchill

Your attitude reflects your state of mind and manifests itself in the manner of your behaviour. It is an extremely accurate barometer of how you truly feel – a barometer that you need to be very aware of. Being able to understand your attitude is a fundamental responsibility of a leader, but it is no easy task.

Attitudes tend to be deeply ingrained in our sub-conscious. Over time they harden and change into opinions which govern our thinking. Attitudes are an amalgam of influences past and present, such as our parents, school and university, our peers, personal experience, religious influence, books, newspapers, television, training, and experience at work. Attitudes change as you gain fresh experience or you become better informed. They become more accurate as you develop insight. Your attitudes are very much a part of your personality; consequently people are always curious to discover what they are. Your attitudes supply intelligence as to how you may react or how you think. This is not necessarily a bad thing, but it is something that you should be conscious of. Be aware that people are as sensitive to attitudes as they are to emotions, and that your attitude will always be registered. As a leader, your attitude to a situation or problem will be very much part of the solution, so it is important that you develop the ability to manage your attitude and to use it to best effect. A positive attitude in a difficult situation, for example, will be picked up very quickly and could have a significant influence on the outcome. As a leader you need to be 'intelligently sympathetic' to the effect your attitude may have on any given situation or encounter.

Are attitudes a fixed state? Definitely not. Of course some of your strongest life influences will always have some bearing on your attitudes, but as they are a state of mind they can be managed and they can be changed. We are all capable of analysing and rationalising our attitudes if we set our minds to it. It's important, therefore, to be aware of our attitudes and to understand why they exist.

Attitude Awareness

Feedback is the most helpful means of making you aware of your attitudes. Self-reflection will also help to uncover them – ask yourself the right questions and be honest about your answers. Examine their causes carefully: they can be very revealing. You may discover that the underlying reason for your attitude is outdated or inappropriate. Be prepared to clear down any competing influences that might have distorted your perspective.

9

What Kind of Leader Are You?

'A leader is a man who has the ability to get other people to do what they don't want to do and like it'
President Truman

Your success as a leader will depend on how you lead. It will depend on your leadership style, your character, and your will to succeed. Your will is something you have within you and is fuelled by your determination. Your character is who you are. Your leadership style will have been developed over time through observation and experience. Through trial and error you will have adopted a style which you believe communicates your message effectively, be it to motivate or to persuade, to give clarity or direction. Your style will have been influenced by the culture of your workplace and by those you have worked for, but are you conscious of what your leadership style *is*? If somebody asked you, what would you say it was? Could you describe it? If you've had some 360 degree feedback you may have an idea, but my guess is that you're probably not sure and may not have even thought about leadership styles.

Consider the way you lead for a moment. Are you happy

with it? Does it produce results? Not sure? Your attitude may well be that if it's worked so far you're happy with the way things are. However, if you want to develop your leadership skills and be an effective leader, it's important that you can identify and use a set of defined leadership styles.

Set out below are six leadership styles which I would like you to consider. Each of these styles represents a particular approach to leadership. You will undoubtedly use elements of each one of them already, but you may not have identified them as individual styles or considered how they might be applied. The styles are:

Inspirational

Coaching

Bonding

Democratic

Commanding

Demanding

Let's look at each one in detail.

Inspirational

Inspirational leaders create vision. They frame the 'big picture' and give direction. They articulate purpose and belonging. They strengthen identity and inspire loyalty. They give clarity and ensure buy-in to the grand design, to new strategies and long-term goals. People feel comforted and motivated by an inspirational leader's enthusiasm and commitment. This style of leadership is particularly useful in times of great change and upheaval.

In such circumstances someone who can point the way, show a way forward and communicate a clear picture of the future is invaluable. Inspirational leaders have presence, they are self-confident, self-aware and good communicators.

Of all the leadership styles, the inspirational style can have the greatest immediate impact. It can be extremely effective and every leader must understand it, perfect it and know when to use it. A couple of things to remember about the inspirational style: it is a 'why' not 'how' style so there are times when this style is not appropriate. Also, if it is used too frequently it will lose its impact – and used on its own it has its limitations. It should be combined with other styles for it to be truly powerful.

Inspirational Skills

'The key to your impact as a leader is your own sincerity. Before you can inspire with emotion, you must be swamped with it yourself. Before you can move to tears, your own must flow. To convince them, you must yourself believe.' This quote by Winston Churchill, one of the world's greatest inspirational leaders, illustrates that for your message to ring true you must genuinely believe in what you say if you are to have credibility. You must believe in what you say and believe in your vision. If you don't, people will pick up on it quickly.

Competent inspirational leaders use empathy. This enables them to articulate their vision effectively and to truly inspire. Sometimes the inspirational leader might employ a little stagecraft as well, but it has to be genuine and honest. Never forget that people derive great comfort from knowing that there is someone who really knows what's going on and can give direction. It is an amazing motivator. Remember that you have to be able to communicate confidence as well as enthusiasm. You have to get your message across whether in the board room or addressing the sales team or the workforce. Inspirational leaders do not hide in their offices and communicate by memo. They get out and about and talk to people. They develop channels of communication to ensure their message gets across unabridged and undiluted. They listen and they ask questions.

Ask yourself the following questions. They've been designed to prompt you and to get you thinking about how you use or could use this style:

- What are the formal lines of communication with your staff? Do they work? How could they be improved?
- What informal lines of communication do you have?
- Do you take time out to talk to people? Do you use these opportunities to share information?
- Do you think your staff know about your vision? Do they share it? Do they believe in it?
- Are you honest with your staff? Do you think they believe that you are?
- Do you think your staff feel part of 'included'? If not, what could you do to change things?
- Do you think you inspire people? Do they believe in you?

Inspirational leaders need to be credible and transparent. They have to steer the ship through rough seas and choose the correct sails when the sun shines and the wind is right. It takes practice, skill and a lot of preparation and thought.

Coaching

A traditional commanding leader might find this style difficult to comprehend, but as with individual coaching it unlocks potential, facilitates performance, learning and development, and is therefore a very powerful tool. Leaders who use a coaching style show a special interest in the development of their staff. It helps them to identify their strengths, and to recognise their weaknesses. By understanding their aspirations and by getting to know them better it helps them establish and share their goals. It is a leadership style that forges a link that will eventually translate into better performance and increased motivation. It might not have an immediate effect on work issues, but it has huge long-term benefits. It is not the most popular style, probably because it requires thought and extra effort, but it enables a leader to connect with people and to open up valuable lines of communication. The quality and accuracy of the feedback you receive will enable you to operate more effectively. It is a style which is as much to do with the heart as it is with the mind. It generates a climate of cooperation and shared interest. It produces clarity. Contrary to popular belief, this style is not time-consuming – in fact it can *save* time – if you have made 'a connection' with your staff it actually reduces time-consuming misunderstandings and confusion.

Nurturing and paying proper attention to those you lead, your valuable human assets, pays huge dividends and is the sign of a truly responsible leader. As with individual coaching, it can have amazingly positive effects on a business's performance.

Coaching Skills

If you have a coach or have had some experience of a coaching management style, you will find that you will be able to understand and use the coaching style very easily.

Coaching can take place in one-to-one meetings or on a more casual basis – you should be alive to spontaneous opportunities to coach. They can be particularly valuable.

Through coaching you can strengthen self-belief and increase awareness and responsibility. 'Listen to understand' and question effectively. Delegate and support. The result will be improved performance and a motivated and focused group of followers. What may seem a very large investment in time is a thoroughly worthwhile investment in human potential which can reap enormous dividends.

Leaders who coach as part of their leadership style, and use the coaching style effectively, have real authenticity.

Bonding

This is a leadership style I would recommend using with caution. Used intelligently it is a powerful and highly effective style, but one that needs to be understood. The aim of the bonding leader is to create harmony. Leaders who use the bonding style do so by building bonds between themselves and their staff, by involving people, by discussing ideas and canvassing opinion. Through encouragement and positive feedback they build trust and encourage initiative. Bonding leaders display sensitivity to people and their feelings, and lend support when it is needed. This way they build morale and create a happy, productive workplace. It creates a feeling of belonging and an atmosphere in which sound working relationships flourish. A climate evolves in which loyalty and commitment are strong. The bonding style is particularly effective when there is a need to increase morale or to repair damage caused when trust has been betrayed.

So what's the downside? This style should never be used exclusively. Its emphasis on positive feedback and lack of corrective feedback can lead to poor performance and a lowering of standards. The absence of direction and advice can be confusing and de-motivating. Leaders can become reluctant to confront reality and may start to worry about whether they are liked or develop a fixation about what people think of them. If they become over-friendly they send confusing signals and create division and discord. The successful use of this style requires sensitivity and sound judgement.

Bonding Skills

Imagine a situation where there has been a breakdown or a betrayal of trust. Morale has sunk to new depths and there is an atmosphere of distrust and disharmony. You arrive on the scene wreathed in smiles and full of good intentions. Your arrival will almost certainly be greeted with suspicion. The message is clear. Apply this style with great care and sensitivity.

Whether you are using the style to repair damage or because you believe it meets the needs of a particular situation, your first task should be to gather intelligence and fully understand the context – background, people, pressures and fears. Observe and listen well. Allow people to know you. Ask for advice, discuss ideas, show interest, be positive, find reason to praise. It will take time, but eventually you will gain enough of people's confidence to begin to build the bonds that will allow you to achieve your goals and make this style work.

Democratic

Cynics might ask what leadership has to do with democracy and be surprised by the answer which is – everything! Leaders cannot isolate themselves from the democratic process. Their success depends on their ability to be good democrats, but how does this translate into a leadership style? Let's examine exactly what the democratic style is and how it works.

The democratic style of leadership is about communication. It's about making a connection to enable you to lead more effectively by actively seeking views and opinions, by asking advice and entertaining new ideas, by getting feedback – good and bad. It is a way of connecting with reality. The effect is to create a feeling of consensus and involvement. People feel that they matter, they feel included. It gives a feeling of collective purpose and commitment. It sounds good and it is – it's a highly effective leadership style, but it has to be used with care.

If you allow it to become your predominant style it can seriously undermine your ability to lead. You need to be able to 'plug in' to it when appropriate and to manage it carefully and sensitively. This requires a lot of practice.

If you come to rely on the democratic style it will become counter-productive. The result is likely to be endless meetings – and then more meetings about meetings. Important decisions will be avoided. People will become unhappy and frustrated, causing confusion and conflict. Consensus will evaporate and your position as leader will have been fatally compromised.

Democratic Skills

What makes a good democratic leader? Good democratic leaders are good communicators and they have excellent listening skills. They take infinite trouble to understand and to know when to ask the right questions, and are not too proud to ask for opinions and to seek advice. They listen to negative feedback and don't shoot the messenger. They are skilled gatherers of intelligence. Through their influence and judgement they use the style to get the best out of people, both by creating a positive culture and by containing conflict. Most importantly, democratic leaders are available and approachable.

The democratic style, used with care and managed with sensitivity, produces a very positive climate within an organisation, but never use it exclusively.

Commanding

Unfashionable? Out-of-date? Effective? Unfashionable maybe, but not to those in the know, definitely not out-of-date, and certainly effective if used at the right time and in the right way.

The commanding style is often associated with the authoritarian command and control management styles of the past, perpetuated by old warhorses and their younger misguided followers. Some leaders who are aware of other leadership styles still use the commanding style in a totally inappropriate manner because 'do as I say' is easy – it's also lazy and harmful. Other less well-informed leaders believe that it is their role to 'tell people what to do'- after all isn't that what being a leader's all about?

When the commanding style is being used badly it's easy to recognise. It's very similar to bullying and it has the same destructive and corrosive effects. It's a world in which commands are issued and immediate unquestioning obedience is demanded. There is an underlying feeling of fear and resentment. This raises stress levels and reduces efficiency. There is an absence of trust and little praise, no cooperation and no motivation. Consequently there is no feedback. Intimidation raises suspicion and constant criticism destroys morale. Soon the first of the disenchanted decides to move on and the ship starts to list.

But does it need to be that way? Certainly not – it should never be that way. So how and when should the commanding style be used? A good example might be in a crisis or in an emergency. This is when the decisive, clear-headed commander comes into his own, giving direction and leadership, taking control and inspiring confidence. Equally the style can be used to get things – and people – moving. To unblock seemingly intractable problems. To drive things forward by being decisive and taking tough decisions, by demonstrating strength and showing resolve. Those who follow you need to have confidence in your ability to 'take command' when it becomes necessary. When you use it in this way and combine it intelligently with other styles, you will gain their respect. A firm, decisive hand on the tiller will also instil confidence and trust in your ability as a leader.

Commanding Skills

Competent commanding leaders have clarity of thought and the ability to control their emotions. These two qualities allow them to keep their feet firmly on the ground. They also develop an instinct about when to use their commanding skills.

Commanding leaders don't ponder over the possible consequences. They take action. They seize the initiative and grasp opportunities, which means being decisive and sufficiently forceful to ensure that things happen. Timing and delivery are absolutely vital. This is a skill which improves with experience, but being self-aware, alert and sensitive to the situation certainly helps. Be aware that when you use this style you are the focus of everyone's attention. If there is hesitation, doubt, or lack of resolve it will be clear for all to see. Show courage and determination and your message will be understood.

Demanding

The clock ticks inexorably towards 8pm and the deadline looms ever closer. There is still a mountain of work to do. Tempers are short. Someone discovers that something has been missed. Your boss returns the work you did that morning and demands a rewrite. Is it the end of the world? It feels like it! You persevere and by midday the following day, having snatched only a couple of hours sleep, you hand in the work two hours ahead of the deadline. Despite your exhaustion you feel relieved and satisfied that you've done a good job – a familiar situation perhaps? There's nothing wrong with a bit of pressure. Working in a fast-moving, pressured environment can be exhilarating and enjoyable, particularly for highly-motivated professionals. Unrelenting pressure however, no matter how stimulating the environment, eventually produces burnout and is highly destructive.

This is why the demanding leadership style should be used with great care. If it is the predominant style of a leader or is used for long periods of time it causes great harm and great unhappiness. If it is a style that you use, please examine carefully how you use it.

Leaders have a responsibility to filter and evaluate the pressures they are under themselves before they pass them on to others. They need to be able to turn up the pressure, to demand more when appropriate or necessary, but they also need to apply the demanding style with caution and sensitivity if they are to achieve the best possible results. So how does it go wrong? Usually when it is used unintelligently and without consideration for its long-term implications. A typical example might be as follows:

EXAMPLE
The leader is ambitious. He wants to impress and takes on new challenges to prove his ability. He willingly puts himself under pressure and insists that his staff follow his example. He demands better results and sets new performance standards. He becomes obsessed with achieving new levels of excellence, and he rewards mistakes, perceived or genuine, with dismissal. The result is that trust evaporates, feedback becomes non-existent and morale disappears. The pressure continues, still the demands increase. Fear and stress fill the air. Eventually the talent leaves to find more fertile pastures, and the leader is left with a de-motivated, unhappy bunch of people. Targets start to be missed, performance drops, recriminations multiply and the leader finds himself friendless and isolated. Slowly the axe begins to fall.....

Demanding Skills

If leadership was all about consensus, bonding, it simply wouldn't be effective. In the real world there are targets to be met, performance levels to be maintained and improved, standards to be raised. A leader needs to be able to show the way, set the pace and steer people's efforts to ensure objectives are achieved. Leaders who use the demanding leadership style effectively will have learnt to use it with great thought and consideration. The fact that they use it at all will be because they have realised that, when used judiciously, it is a valuable means of improving performance and making the most of opportunities. Leaders have high personal standards and demand similar standards from those they lead – not an unreasonable demand – but they would be well advised to use the demanding style sparingly and judiciously if they want to be really effective.

Leaders are always in pursuit of excellence. Enlightened leaders realise that true excellence is seldom achieved. A blind belief that it can be achieved if the pressure is maintained will always lead to disappointment. It is a style that has to be measured, understood, and thoughtfully applied if real results are to be achieved.

Application

So what type of leader are you? Inspirational? Of course! Coaching? Not sure? Bonding? It has been known. Democratic? Maybe. Commanding? All too often! Demanding? Always! Give the question some thought.

I hope that you have found the explanation of each of the styles helpful. Now you are aware of what they are and what they consist of, compare them to the style you use. You probably use elements of each of the styles already, but perhaps there's quite a lot that is new to you. I recommend you familiarise yourself with the styles and work out which ones you feel most comfortable with. Those that are less familiar you should study and understand, because you should be able to use all six. A skilled leader will know when and in what manner each style should be applied, and will have the ability to combine styles and use elements of others in order to meet the needs of the situation or the task.

As an exercise, think of a recent situation you had to deal with which involved using your skill as a leader. Now write down which of the six leadership skills you would have used if you were faced with the same situation. Ask yourself when you would have applied them, and in what manner. What combinations would have been most effective? Now compare what you think the likely outcome would be with what actually happened. What do you notice ? I hope the first thing you noticed was that you spent more time considering the styles you thought would be suitable and that you were more careful in your approach. With practice, it becomes instinctive. It's a good feeling! Your reward for mastering the effective use of the leadership styles will be increased self-confidence and personal effectiveness – and a deeper loyalty and commitment from those you lead.

PART TWO

REALITY

Reality

'Who is it that can tell me who I am?'
King Lear, Act 1, Scene 4

Leadership is a people business. That might appear to be a blindingly obvious statement, but take a look around you. How many leaders realise that? I'm sure that you've met some whose interpersonal skills are non-existent: you might be suffering at the hands of one right now! They might have IQ's in the stratosphere: they may have been trained in the best business schools and be thoroughly competent, but they're not good leaders. When I meet people like that I'm always reminded of a remark made on the drill square at Sandhurst by a Scots Guards Sergeant Major who had been less than impressed by the performance of a certain officer cadet on the previous day's field exercise. Staring straight into the eyes of this poor unfortunate, their faces centimetres apart, he says very deliberately, *'As for you sir, I wouldn't follow you, not even out of curiosity!'*

When we examine great leaders, be they famous political figures or highly motivated entrepreneurs, they often seem the most unlikely characters, but there's something special about them. Their IQ may well be above average, but there's something else – invariably they are emotionally intelligent. Emotional intelligence is the special ingredient. It makes the difference, it makes them special. It contributes enormously to their success. Therefore your ability to be an effective leader is not determined solely by your IQ score – which is based on logical reasoning – but also on your being emotionally literate. Effective leadership depends to a significant extent on your ability to tune in to, and understand, emotional states.

You need to able to use and understand the emotional intelligence competencies of self-awareness, self-management, self-responsibility, relationship management and intelligent leadership styles as well – this is what Part 1 is all about.

Now I want to explore the reality of leadership and how it affects *you*.

1

Reality Check

> *'Leadership is first learning then doing'*
> **Alistair Mant**

In the introduction to this book I said that reality was the currency of leadership. The reality I would now like you to think about is *you*. I want you to take ten paces back and take a good look at yourself. Who is this person you see in front of you? Do you see an ambitious go-getter fulfilling life's destiny, clear in the knowledge that you know what motivates you, or do you see someone eager to succeed but uncertain if you have the will to make it happen? Do you see someone who really knows what they want and believes they have the ability to succeed, or someone filled with self-doubt wondering whether they're in the right job? Is that person in front of you totally focused and happy in their role, clear about their values, or someone wondering what the whole thing is all about? Be honest with yourself.

I'd like you to treat this exercise as a further step in building your self-awareness. This time the focus is on more specific aspects of your life. Some of these questions may be ones that you avoided asking yourself in your moments of self-reflection and you may feel a little uncomfortable at the prospect of addressing them, but they are fundamental if you are to make progress and achieve your goal of becoming an effective leader. The questions should test your self-belief as well so they're pretty important – after all if you don't believe in you, is it fair to ask anyone else to?

The three questions are about Drive, Desire and Values. So where do you stand?

Drive

What really drives you? Why do you get out of bed in the morning? Why do you go the extra mile? What motivates you to want to succeed? Do you believe that you can? If your answers are, for example, that you want to do the best job possible, you're fascinated by the job you do, doing the job well makes you feel good, what you do interests you, you want to be an effective leader, then you know you're on the right side of the line. Even better if you believe that you want to make a difference, to make a positive contribution – through your efforts to make the world a better place. If on the other hand you believe that you have something to prove, either to yourself or to others, then beware! If your purpose is to show you can make a lot of money or that you can be CEO just like your father, then this is the territory where reality becomes distorted and effective leadership becomes difficult. It may not end in failure, but it can lead to a lot of unhappiness, for you and for others. You'll not be a leader people will willingly want to follow – even out of curiosity!

Desire

Do you *really* want to make things happen? Do you have a vision? Do you have the desire to make a difference? If you do then you need the will to make that a reality and to believe in yourself. This isn't something that can be taught, although we all have the desire in us in varying measures. It is a very natural way of self-expression – but it needs to be activated. I think the word *passion* may be a more evocative word to use. It's more powerful than a desire or a want. Whatever the case, do you have the passion, the hunger to lead or are you filled with self-doubt? If there's doubt you need to address it. As a leader you need to believe in what you're doing and have a passion to make it happen. How can you create a vision for those you lead if you don't? You certainly can't if you're filled with doubt – whatever it may be. If you doubt you will ask questions, but probably not press for answers. You will fear success as much as you fear failure. Not the stuff leaders are made of.

Values

Ask yourself what your true values are. Integrity? Honesty? Fairness? Compassion? Family? Service? Truth? As an exercise, write down your values and then put them in order of priority. Consider them for a moment. Are you true to your values? Do you live by them? Do you think about them or do you need a simple exercise like this to make you aware of them?

I would suggest that knowing, understanding and maintaining your values should be one of your top priorities. If you believe in your values, and hold them dear, then you should never allow them to be compromised. Sometimes the influence and culture of the organisation you work for can put your beliefs under severe pressure. The temporary influence of others or an organisational matter can also cloud reality. When this happens, it's decision time for you. If you want to be a good leader you have to have integrity, and be honest with yourself and honest with others. Ask yourself if there's there a good match between your values and that of the organisation you work for. There should be. Are you comfortable about the decisions that you are asked to take? If you can't sign up to what is being asked of you then there are choices that need to be made. Fail to make the right one and it could affect your future as a leader. Remember that these are fundamental issues. Compromise as far as value issues are concerned is at best unwise and at worst disastrous. Stand by what you believe in, act accordingly and you will gain respect from those you lead. Of course not everything is as black and white as I have painted it here, but let your conscience be the guardian of your values, and have the courage of your convictions.

Drive, Desire and Values are three things that you need to understand about yourself: they are your reality. They are not fixed in stone – they can change – but in order to be in tune with yourself, and with others, you need to be aware of them and to understand them.

2

Goals Revisited

> *'Live as if you were to die tomorrow. Learn as if you were going to live forever'*
> **Mahatma Gandhi**

Life is not a dress rehearsal. There can be no truer statement. This is it. No second chances. None of us can foretell what life holds in store for us, so we owe it to ourselves to give it our best shot. We need to escape what I call the 'Rap Trap':

$$\mathbf{R}\text{outine} = \mathbf{A}\text{pathy} = \mathbf{P}\text{aralysis}$$

Cast off the suffocating blanket of routine and become passionate about life! Discover your dreams and look to the future with enthusiasm. Right now perhaps you are examining your current routine, and the trials, tribulations and frustrations of your existence are parading themselves before you – but don't despair! There *is* a way out, there *is* a way forward, but *you* have to be the catalyst. For things to change you have to *make* things happen. If you wait for things to happen chances are they won't – or you could be waiting a very long time. I can pretty much guarantee that you will be disappointed.

If you have produced a learning plan – which was mentioned in Part 1 under 'Self-development' – you will have made a very good start. The process will have gone some way to help you understand what you really want to be and to discover your 'ideal self'. To use a theatrical analogy, you have studied the part, learnt your lines and you are now going to give a virtuoso performance. What comes next is to identify your vision and to ignite your passion. To connect with your enthusiasm you are going to make some changes. It's all up to you. Yes, it's all about 'change'. Breaking old habits, slaughtering sacred cows, concentrating on the race not the next hurdle. It's about having proper 'goals' that encapsulate your vision and harbour your dreams. Goals that will bring clarity, purpose and meaning to your life. They are an essential part of your development as an emotionally intelligent leader.

Taking Stock

To have really meaningful goals in your life it's important that you understand exactly who you are. I mean who you are now, who you *actually* are. What sort of leader you are, what sort of person you are, what excites you, what bores you, what your true talents are, what you believe in. I suggest that you revisit the exercises you did in the Self-image section in Part 1 and dig a little deeper. Examine the person you see in the mirror every morning – and I mean the rather unattractive apparition that greets you just after you've just crawled out of bed, not the groomed sophisticate setting out to conquer the world. If you haven't done this exercise for some time and you do it thoroughly and honestly, you will probably find it quite a challenge. You will have changed. Time will have concealed these changes from you. Daily life and a grinding routine will have had its effect. Revisit the roads you have travelled. Examine your influences, good and bad. Relive your experiences and question the lessons that you heeded and the ones you ignored. It may be that you may not like what you discover, but remember the true purpose is to try and establish a clear understanding of your 'true self', however painful.

Reflect on the person you thought you were and contrast it with the person you are now.

This exercise is to enable you to fully understand your 'real self' so that the goals that you set for yourself are themselves 'real'. As a suggestion you might consider having a discussion with your coach. It may help you to uncover and understand hidden uncomfortable truths about yourself, and reveal your forgotten strengths.

Identifying Your Goals

If you feel that your personal 'reality check' is complete and that you have a clear and honest understanding of who you are, you should re-examine and reset your goals. I hope that once you have established what they are you will consider that they are more realistic, clearer and that you feel happier to own them.

There have been many studies carried out to determine the value of goal setting. They all point to the fact that setting specific, well-thought-through goals produces results.

It therefore makes sense that you think long and hard about your goals.

I would suggest that you concentrate on the goals that are most important to you in your working and personal life. Split them into long- and short-term goals that reflect your personal philosophy and your values, your aspirations and your ambitions. If these are clear and genuine then you will have a strong foundation on which to build your future. You will also have a clear understanding of what you want to be and what you want to achieve.

You may find **YOURS** useful when you come to consider your goals:

Your: Goals should be **your** goals, determined by you and by nobody else.

Objective: Your goals should have an **objective**, a clear and measurable purpose which you believe in 100 per cent.

Understandable: Goals should be clear, **understandable**, specific and unambiguous.

Realistic: Goals should be **realistic** – not wishful or unattainable.

Strengths: Base all your goals on your **strengths** not your weaknesses.

I have made a strong case for the need to establish goals. You will doubtless meet those who believe that they are an unnecessary straightjacket and restrict freedom of manoeuvre and creative thought. I would argue that they do exactly the opposite and that they are fundamental. They enable leaders to have a vision of what they want their ideal lives to be. They allow them the freedom to be creative and to design plans to achieve them. They create focus, foster passion and help to make dreams come true.

(See Goal Planner, Appendix B; and Goal Report, Appendix C.)

3

A Foundation for Effective Leadership

'If your actions inspire others to dream more, to do more, and become more, you are a leader'
John Quincy Adams

Throughout your life as you learn, as you gain experience, as you grow, your dreams and your aspirations will change. The goals you have set need to accommodate these changes. Far from being a straightjacket, goals should be flexible and reflect your 'real self'. They should reflect any new-found strengths, but above all they need to represent current reality. As a responsible leader you need to maintain that reality. This is best done by being self-aware and by active self-management. This process should become a part of your life. You need to 'keep connected' and maintain your vision if you want to get the best out of life and inspire others to follow you.

Maintaining Focus

Whether we like it or not we all experience disruption and

unexpected change in our lives. Today continuity and certainty, tomorrow disaster and disappointment! Whatever the ups and downs in our personal or professional lives, it is important to maintain focus. This is not easy to do even in good times – in tough times it is twice as hard. Leaders with a clear vision, who are clear about their goals, who are self-aware, who know themselves, are better equipped to maintain focus and offer positive and constructive leadership than those who are not. Courage, determination, decisiveness and clear thinking is what will be demanded of you, and as an effective leader this is exactly what you must deliver. To do this, those you lead must share your vision. They need to share your sense of purpose and direction if they are to assist you in maintaining focus.

We live in a competitive, knowledge-based world. The organisations we work for are lean and flat. Layers of management have been peeled away. The new shape of these organisations has dramatically changed the working environment in general and the role of the leader in particular. Leadership has replaced management and learning has replaced instruction. The relationship between boss and subordinate, the social glue that held organisations together, has all but melted. The way we do business has changed – the pace of business has quickened. These realities require a new approach to leadership. As I have stressed previously, effective leadership now depends in great part on being able to tune into emotional states. Knowing one's emotions, managing one's emotions, motivating oneself, recognising emotions in others, handling relationships, all these are vital skills in the armoury of the effective and emotionally intelligent leader.

The old command structure has been replaced with by a culture of persuasion and consent. Authority does not come with title, it has to *earned*. Leaders have to be competent and lead by example, encouraging and helping those they lead to do their jobs better. Your ability to engage with the emotional reality of your organisation and those that you lead is of paramount importance.

In Part One 'Discovery', I have mapped out, as a foundation, some of the essential competencies and practical applications which apply to emotionally intelligent leadership. Part Two 'Reality', is all about you. I hope you now have a clearer picture of who you are and what you would like your ideal self to be, and that you now have clearly defined short- and long-term goals. I would like to go on to address some of the more practical aspects of being an effective and emotionally intelligent leader.

PART THREE

PRACTICE

Practice

'It is a time for a new generation of leadership to cope with new problems and new opportunities. For there is a new world to be won'
John F Kennedy

John F. Kennedy's statement referred to a bygone era, but it is just as true of today's world. There *are* new problems and there *are* new opportunities. There *is* a new world to be won, an exciting one that has undergone profound social, economic and technological changes. A world that has to cope with continuous and ever-increasing change, an information revolution, a huge growth in computer power, and a dramatic increase in the pace and the manner in which business is done. This is a world of facts, figures, analysis and comparison, of pressure and performance; where your competitor is not next-door but on the other side of the world. A world where no quarter is given, but which abounds with new opportunities. Where no leader can be omnipotent. Where yesterday's dynamo is today's dinosaur and the tyranny of the tall pyramid has become a part of history. The vacuum in which yesterday's leaders operated has imploded. Information is no longer power, it is common currency.

The effects of these changes have been fundamental as far as leadership practices are concerned. Whilst the rules of leadership have not changed, the practice and the application have. In some cases it's a question of emphasis, in others a return to basics. Essential basics that had been buried and forgotten in an era dominated by myopic authoritarians – seasoned practitioners in the command school of leadership – or just fallen into disuse. Today, in addition to reviving the basics, there are the new skills: a new 'knowledge' which needs to be acquired and understood for the new organisations to function effectively. This 'knowledge' I have set out in Parts One and Two: the *intra*personal skills – tuning into *yourself*, self-awareness, self-understanding, self-management and self-responsibility, and the *inter*personal skills – how you relate, understand, respond and work with *others* – in other words emotional intelligence. Put more formally: 'To be able to recognise, perceive and sense emotions in yourself and in others. To use that knowledge to assist thought and understanding and as a source of information, influence, creativity, and energy'.

I hope that you now have an understanding of what is required to be an emotionally intelligent leader, and the enormous benefits to you and to others that this knowledge brings.

1

People

> *'The best executive is the one who has the sense to pick good men to do what he wants done, and the self-restraint to keep from meddling with them while they do it'*
> **Theodore Roosevelt**

People are an appreciating asset – or at least they *should* be. The more they are nurtured, trained and developed, the more valuable they become to you and to your organisation. Your task as a leader is to create an environment in which they can flourish – to develop a healthy and dynamic culture which allows them to progress from just doing a job of work to making a very real contribution. They need to feel that they belong and to believe that what they are doing makes a difference. They need to feel they are involved, no matter what their role. A connection needs to be made between you and those you lead. It should be real and it should be meant. This can be done by addressing their needs and their aspirations, *and* by sharing yours with them. How successful you are will very much depend upon how skilful you are at creating bonds which are respected and valued. Remember that you are only as good as those who support you.

With leadership comes responsibility. Your first responsibility is not to yourself or to your organisation, but to those whom you are privileged to lead. This is one of the forgotten basics which in the recent past has lead to a very selfish, unhappy and inefficient culture within many organisations. Being responsible means caring, understanding, being involved. Making the extra effort. Putting the interests of others before your own. Emotionally intelligent illiterates find this concept difficult to understand. They consider it naïve in a competitive world. It is, however, what leadership has always been about, and today it is even more important. Emotionally intelligent leaders understand that people come first.

The Right People

Recruiting the right people is so important. This may seem a very obvious statement, but it is a sad fact of life that many leaders abdicate responsibility when it comes to the process of recruitment. It can, after all, be a very tedious and time-consuming task. It always seems to figure low down on the list of priorities even when the need is great. Consider the scenario: A far-off HR department is given the task of finding a replacement in your department. The brief they are given may be adequate, but has probably not been given the time and thought that it should have. The result is a pile of uninspiring and unsuitable CVs, a series of tiring and pointless interviews, followed by having to make a choice from an unconvincing shortlist. Going through the exercise all over again is not an option because of time and cost. You end up recruiting second best.

Recruitment is something effective leaders pay a lot of attention to. Second best should never be allowed to be an option. Unfortunately many organisations have very formalised recruiting policies which can be frustrating to the diligent leader eager to recruit the best. If you're unable to change the system or to influence it in any way, start by doing the following:

- Know what you want.
- Identify the role, and discuss and confirm it with others.
- Identify specific qualities you are looking for.
- Write the job specification personally. Pay attention to key words.
- Satisfy yourself that your requirement is understood.
- See as many CVs as you can – get involved in the sifting process.
- If you are not doing the initial interviews yourself, thoroughly brief those who are.
- Research your short list. Ensure you take references.
- Take time over the interviews. Be painstaking. Involve others. Ask penetrating questions.
- Never compromise – trust your instincts.

It may be that your organisation insists on some form of psychometric testing such as Myers Briggs or its equivalent. It could be part of the service offered by the recruitment company. How you view these tests is very much a personal thing, and whether you use or value them will depend on how they have worked for you in the past. They can be incredibly useful and they can sometimes be misleading. You will have your own experience. There are now several Emotional Intelligence assessment tools available and they offer a new and different perspective. Here are a selection:

The Seligman Attributional Style Questionnaire (SASQ)

The Bar-On Emotional Quotient Inventory (EQ-I)

The Emotional Intelligence Questionnaire (EIQ)

The EQ Map (Q-Metrics)

Remember, the CV might indicate a close match to your requirement. Qualifications could be blindingly impressive, but the EI score could be disastrous. You might never know. Better to know before it's too late. I would suggest that if you haven't used an Emotional Intelligence assessment tool before, it might be well worth trying.

Recruiting someone new should always be treated sensitively. If you are over-enthusiastic about the appointment you have made, you will create suspicion and resentment. Consultation, discussion and the sensitive introduction of potential candidates before an appointment is made can sometimes make the acceptance process easier for all parties. Acceptance is what we all want when we join a new group. Unfortunately, behind the welcoming smile there are often other agendas. Are you a threat? Will you make a positive contribution? Where do your weaknesses lie? How far can you be pushed? Do you have a sense of humour? How seriously do you take yourself? What is your ambition? How good are you at your job? Natural human curiosity occurs in any organisation. If the new appointment has been handled with care it will go a long way to ensuring that this natural curiosity does not manifest itself in any negative or harmful fashion. How someone new is accepted and treated is always a good indication of the emotional maturity of those you lead.

Getting to Know You

"Getting to know you, getting to know all about you..." Have you? How well do you know the people you lead? For example, would you know if one of your direct reports spends all her spare time looking after her disabled mother? Would you know if another was going through a painful divorce? Would you know if you had a former junior tennis champion on your staff? You might if you'd taken the time to find out. Knowing about the people you lead is one of those forgotten leadership basics which is fundamental to effective leadership. Your knowledge should be current as well as historical. If one of your direct reports – or the tea lady for that matter – has a problem which they are prepared to share, then you should know about it – not so that you can just be seen to be interested or because you think that it's the sort of thing that a leader should do, but because you are *genuinely* interested and want to help if you can. Know them well so that you can share their joys and their successes too. This involves spending time with people, real time. Take time out with people to get to find out more about them, to know them better (this means more than an occasional drink after work). In the process they will know you better and as a result you will gain their respect and loyalty. This is about using your leadership skills – your bonding skills in particular. Learn to ask the right questions. Remember things about people, their likes and dislikes, where they spend their holidays, what age their children are. It's important that *you* do because it's important to *them*.

As an exercise, write down all you know about two of your direct reports. How much do you know about them? Make a list of questions. If you score yourself low then you've got work to do. It's up to you. Remember, those you lead spend their time supporting you, so make sure you support them. This is not tiresome detail, it's hugely important.

Keeping in Touch

Information is power. Withholding or filtering information is power too. Leaders need accurate information, intelligence if you like, if they are to be successful and if they are to be effective. They need information 'flow': accurate sources and means of gathering. Developing different ways of obtaining information (and I don't mean setting up spy networks or having informers!) is very important. The best information is obtained by having the trust of those you lead, where information is readily given without any fear of recrimination. A self-aware leader who has built up respect and trust with those he leads – who uses the bonding and coaching styles of leadership – is more likely to have a free flow of information, and as a result be more effective.

Information vacuums occur when information is handled carelessly. Leaders who shoot the messenger will suffer a quiet, information-free life. Leaders who fail to understand the sensitivity of the information they are given will lose trust and become isolated. Their direct reports will become economical with the truth, frugal with the facts.

People are just as sensitive to the way you react to information they give you as they are to your moods or emotions. They notice what you do with it, how you handle it, what use you make of it. Their motives might be to ensure that they are not put at risk by the way you handle the information they give you or what you do with it. No matter how hungry for information the leader may be, or how reliable the source, all information should be treated with care. There are those who are always happy to feed the leader with information, but who may have another agenda or be influenced by the bias of self-interest. All information and all sources should be scanned for viruses and judged by the quality of the information they provide.

Information in its broadest sense lubricates creative thought. By keeping in touch through active questioning and careful listening, information will flow and ideas will follow.

Feedback is one of the most effective means of keeping in touch. It can be freely given or it can be canvassed. However, finding ways of obtaining accurate feedback is not always easy and it can sometimes lack essential honesty. Properly conducted, using multiple sources, it can provide a fuller and more complete picture, and widen the perspective. It is useful to remember that the intelligence community do not consider intelligence to be either accurate or reliable unless it has been verified by *at least two sources.*

The purpose of emphasising the need to 'keep in touch' is to highlight, particularly to newly-appointed leaders, the danger of allowing your position to become an information-free zone, the need to be on your guard about the quality of the information you are fed, and the importance of working hard at improving your flow of information. Question, listen, ask for feedback, canvass opinion, discuss and debate. There is no excuse for being ill-informed.

Developing Others

It is no coincidence that successful organisations have a strong leadership development culture. They recognise that the future of their organisation depends upon their ability to successfully nurture and cultivate tomorrow's leaders. Essentially these are learning organisations and, as such, will spend a significant amount of time and energy promoting a learning culture. Emotionally intelligent leaders, whether they are fortunate enough to work for such organisations or not, also recognise the need to establish a culture which promotes learning and leadership development. They understand that they too must invest a significant amount of their time in the development of those they lead if they are to achieve their aims. An emotionally intelligent leader is all too aware that things that matter are rarely achieved alone.

Leadership development is more than seeing that people attend the right courses, that their skills and knowledge is updated – although that aspect is important. It is about understanding their strengths and weaknesses, identifying areas where they excel and ones where they perform poorly. It is about allowing and helping them to *grow and learn while they work.*

As a leader you have a duty of care. This takes commitment. A leadership development programme is time-consuming. It's also hard work. Beware that when the pressure is on it can easily slide down the list of priorities and be forgotten. It's too important to allow that to happen. Think ahead and ensure your schedule is designed to accommodate your programme. Try and make this time sacred. Don't allow time thieves to steal it.

Plan your programme. Map out your objectives. Think of ways of achieving these objectives and tools that you can use. The bonding and coaching leadership styles can be used to great effect in the development of people. They help to forge links and promote better understanding. So what's the best way to use these styles? What are the key elements of a successful development programme? What do you need to do? The first thing is to:

Observe

Listen

Evaluate

Observing, listening and evaluating is actually an on-going process which should become second nature to you.

Observe and listen. **Listen** to what is *not* being said as well as what is. You will discover how people are performing, what needs to be improved. It will highlight shortcomings and reveal opportunities. It will identify star performers and prompt you to find ways of developing them further. It will uncover those who are eclipsed by the rising stars and require special attention. Perhaps they need to be given a fresh sense of purpose or put in a position where their talents could be better used. You will become aware of competencies which are lacking or need improvement.

Evaluate what you observe and hear. Consider the implications and discuss it with those concerned. Ask for comments and advice. Focus your attention. Invest your time. Next:

Identify
Train
Encourage

Identify priorities. Identify special requirements. Identify individual needs. Identify sound and realistic courses of action which will produce positive results.

Train. Sit down and discuss development goals with individuals. Agree these goals. Make sure they are **SMART** goals: Specific, Measured, Agreed, Realistic and Time-phased. Spend time ensuring that the goals set really are appropriate and will contribute to the development of the individual or individuals concerned. Ensure the goals are understood and 'owned'. Make sure they are met, and give help and advice if difficulties are encountered. Monitor and measure.

Encourage. Encouragement is such a powerful motivator. Use it intelligently and it will have a significant impact on performance. Offer guidance. Inspire and motivate. Give a sense of purpose and share your visions.

True development can really only take place in a positive atmosphere, where exploration and adventure are encouraged and where mistakes are forgiven – when they are understood and lessons are learnt. This type of atmosphere does not suddenly appear or evolve. It has to be designed and championed by you. For it to work you have to demonstrate unequivocal encouragement and support for the individuals concerned. They must understand your commitment to their learning. Inconsistency in your reactions will fracture this process irrevocably and breed doubt and fear. It will destroy your ability to encourage development.

A learning culture, in which meaningful development can take place, has to be fostered and driven by you. If you are impatient you will be disappointed. If you are patient, committed and conscientious about developing the people you lead, you can look forward to your assets increasing in value and a high-dividend yield.

The Benefits of a Coaching Culture

I make no apologies for moving straight from 'developing others' to 'the benefits of a coaching culture' because I believe coaching is such an important development tool. Why? Because coaching offers a unique link, a means to help people understand their values and abilities. To identify their strengths and weaknesses. To establish their goals and to formulate a plan for achieving them. It allows you to get to know people on a much more personal level. To make a vital connection which can uncover hidden talents as well as giving you practical feedback and creative input.

The establishment of a coaching ethos requires not only a commitment from you, but also for you to demonstrate your *belief in the process*. It needs to be seen to work and for others to experience and understand the benefits. This will take time to establish, but when it is, it will greatly enhance your ability to lead effectively and to achieve the goal of every emotionally intelligent leader: *to successfully develop others*.

Let's examine once again a definition of coaching:

> 'Coaching is unlocking a person's potential to maximise their performance and to help them develop and learn in the process.'

Why can coaching be so effective? Well, for a start it is generally non-directive and non-judgemental. No telling, no instructing. A process of asking questions and actively listening. If you are a self-aware leader who is able to empathise well, coaching can have a very positive emotional impact. It allows you to establish a relationship with those you lead and communicates the fact that you have their interests at heart, that you believe in them, and above all, that you care. It soon creates an atmosphere in which people believe they are valued, and as a result their self-confidence improves and their performance increases.

A coaching culture sits well with the new reality of consensus and higher performance – *because it works*. As a leadership style, it has become an essential part of a leader's repertoire – not used exclusively, but individually or in conjunction with others. Today coaching is also an accepted management style. The coaching style of management has been described as a more holistic way of management. It has evolved from the success of individual and team coaching in business and in sport. It is also a logical response to the need for more openness and to the change in business culture. Its introduction has helped to weaken the blame culture which has existed in many organisations for far too long. It has built awareness by allowing people to accept and take responsibility for their actions. Its prime benefit, however, has been to promote development and to make it the main focus of the process. Better performance has been the result.

Dealing with Conflict

Just as the sun doesn't always shine, so peace, harmony and concord don't always exist in the workplace. Effective leadership, particularly when the bonding and democratic styles of leadership are used in the correct measure and at the appropriate time, should be able to identify the seeds of conflict and ensure that the matter is addressed and not allowed to escalate. The use of the coaching style can help to exorcise potential problems by increasing awareness and getting those concerned to accept and understand their responsibilities. Dialogue and the free flow of information will prevent misunderstandings. Nevertheless conflict *will* arise, and when it does it has to be dealt with promptly and effectively, and should not be allowed to fester. You do not want to spend your time chasing after escaped conflicts!

The origins of conflict can be simple and they can be complicated. They can be contrived. They can arise from a simple misunderstanding or from misinterpretation. They can involve a clash of personalities or a conflict of interests. Whatever the case, their origins must be uncovered and understood if the conflict is to be resolved.

Dealing with conflict, either at home or at work, is something we do frequently in our lives. A conflict of any sort is usually always looked upon as being 'a problem' and is regarded as being negative. It may well be, but for a diligent leader who is not prepared to accept any conflict at face value, there is always wealth of information – positive *and* negative – to be assessed. It can uncover problems. It can prompt possibilities. It can reveal strengths and weaknesses in your organisation and in those you lead. It can tell you where you're going wrong, what area you need to pay attention to, how successful you are as a leader. It can help identify important issues. If you approach dealing with conflict with a positive and open mind and don't allow anger, irritation and frustration to cloud your vision – in other words if you manage your emotions – you will find that there is much to gain. Never forget that *every problem has the seeds of its own solution.*

Perhaps your success as a leader should not be judged by the way you deal with conflict, but in your ability to create a culture where conflict is rare. Utopia? Not really. In an emotionally intelligent organisation there should be less reason for conflict to arise. There will always be conflict of course, but it should be rare, and your task as an emotionally intelligent leader is to make sure that this is the case. To do so you need to be an 'authentic' leader and for those you lead to recognise that this is what you are. The core quality of an authentic leader is honesty. Honesty attracts trust and in conflict resolution this is an essential ingredient.

In any organisation there will be situations that occur which generate discussion and debate. These can lead to conflict. All organisations contain diverse individuals with a variety of experience and with widely differing ambitions. When the glue that holds these individuals together comes unstuck, your task is to put it together again. No temporary fix! It should be a permanent and long-lasting repair. Which requires you not to allow your emotions to interfere with the process. I would suggest you try the **REPAIR** procedure:

Reveal the differences between the parties.

Expose the reasons for the conflict.

Provide a platform to uncover the perspectives.

Acknowledge feelings.

Identify common ground and shared ideals.

Redirect energies.

Reveal the differences between the parties. Discover the differing viewpoints. Fully understand them. If you do not you will have little chance of resolving the conflict. You need to be seen to understand what these differences are and for there to be *no ambiguity*. Spend time on this – it will be time well-spent.

Expose the reasons for the conflict. These may not be what they seem. They may not be what you are told. Question thoroughly and get to the truth. The truth may be uncomfortable for one (or both) of the parties so tread carefully. It may be a question of personalities and not of fact. If the reason for the conflict is understood by both parties a positive resolution is more likely.

Provide a platform to uncover perspectives. Provide opportunity for discussion. Get to the nub of the matter. Find out the perspectives of both parties. This will uncover misunderstandings and misinterpretations. Examine / discuss the differences. Ask questions – empathise. Gather information, notice emotions, discover feelings, uncover thoughts, understand assumptions. Question sensitively and thoughtfully, and don't be judgemental or show any bias in your reaction.

Acknowledge feelings. It does not pay to be unsympathetic to either party's feelings and they should understand that this is your attitude. Cooperation will be the result. Your attitude should be friendly but purposeful.

Identify common ground and shared ideals. In any conflict situation there are shared ideals to be exposed and usually there is a lot of common ground. Once identified, a way forward can be found. Stress and anxiety may well have closed down the otherwise open channels to creative thinking. By identifying a common purpose, which reduces tension and brings both parties together, it is far more likely that the solution to the conflict will be found.

Redirect energies. Conflict resolution does not succeed if there are seen to be winners and losers. One party might be wrong. The other may have had some justification in bringing matters to a head. What is really important is that *both* parties need to go away feeling better, with a positive frame of mind and having a fresh resolve. To do this requires skill, patience and determination on the part of the leader, as well as a great deal of creative thinking – which can often be exhausting. Don't look upon conflicts as a waste of your time. They can be an unwelcome distraction, but they have immense value. Take time out to reflect on what took place. See if there are lessons to be learnt and whether you need to take any further action. Monitor the parties concerned to ensure the conflict does not resurface.

Use your coaching leadership skills in resolving conflict. Use the opportunity to reduce any interferences that might become apparent to you. Remember: '**Potential** minus **Interferences** equals **Performance**'. Make sure you fully understand each party's point of view. Reframe the problem and offer a new perspective if this is appropriate. Lastly, never miss an opportunity to inspire and enthuse.

2

Communication

'The most powerful way to connect to another person is to listen. Just listen. Perhaps the most important thing we ever give each other is our attention'
Rachel Remen

Speech, body language, demeanour, attitude, language, expression, feel, smell, touch, hearing, sight, personality, looks, gestures, the way we dress, the company we keep – these are only some of the many means we use to communicate. But how well do we use them? Our proficiency depends upon many things, on our environment, our experience, habits, our needs and desires, our sensitivity – and on *practice*.

The information we receive through our eyes and our ears through touch and smell is evaluated by both our *thinking* brain and our *emotional* brain. It is evaluated instantaneously together with past experience, memories, beliefs, feelings, thoughts and ideas. The result is an emotional response – a summary if you like, which we then have to interpret. The result may be translated into action or no action as the situation requires, which then becomes part of our accumulated 'wisdom'. The more emotionally intelligent we become – particularly the more self-aware we are – the better we are at interpreting these emotions. The more reasoned and appropriate our responses are, the more able we are to employ our accumulated wisdom effectively.

Listening

Listening is a skill. Along with the ability to question effectively, it is one of the key communication skills. Most of us miss out on so much because we don't listen properly. We *hear* everything, but we *listen* selectively. Misunderstandings occur more through poor or careless listening than through the quality or content of what is actually being said. We are keener to talk, to voice our opinion than we are to listen. We have created arenas where we can propound our theories: 'talking shops' where we can expound our ideas and our opinions, 'think tanks' where we talk a lot and think a little. We are enveloped in a thick cloud of words floating on a thermal of hot air. Talking is good, but if we don't listen and listen effectively, words become meaningless and a waste of time and effort.

Jousting with words is what most of us practise. Sometimes we hit the mark, but mostly our efforts are fruitless. We emphasise or punctuate our speech with dramatic statements to get attention; we use expletives to try and make our point because we know that people don't listen properly. We are impatient. Our attention span has diminished so dramatically that we have little time for involved dialogue or long conversations. We communicate in a succession of headline statements which communicate fact and feeling, but often very little meaning.

To learn, to progress, to be effective, we *have* to become good communicators. Good leaders are good communicators. Good communicators are good listeners. We have to learn to listen.

Instinctively we all know when someone isn't listening. It's very frustrating and extremely annoying. Leaders who don't listen become isolated and out of touch. Why waste time on someone who doesn't listen? Gradually they loose touch with reality and with those they lead, and eventually they become ineffective.

Paying attention and listening to someone is really a common courtesy. Not to listen is discourteous and insulting, particularly if it is made obvious. No matter how senior you become, no matter how important you think you are, no matter how unimportant you consider what is being said or who is saying it, you should always listen. It is a mark of the sort of person you are and of how effective you are as a leader. By showing interest people will warm to you and want to communicate with you.

Listening can be difficult. For example, what is being said might be nonsense and the person saying it maybe someone whose opinions you distrust or disagree with. The speaker's delivery might be appalling. You may have other important business on your mind. These are good excuses for not listening, but regardless of the circumstances it is a very bad idea to allow yourself to become judgemental or to be distracted without listening first. Avoid starting habits which will be difficult to break.

Let's examine the four states of listening:

Not listening

Half listening

Listening to reply

Listening to understand

Not listening. You are there in body, but not in mind. Your thoughts are somewhere else. If you were asked to summarise what had just been said, you wouldn't be able to. If you were asked what you had been thinking about you would probably be able to give a detailed and clear account. It would have been obvious to any observer that you had not been listening, both because of your body language and by your expression.

Half listening. You register the topic of the conversation. Your interest wanes. You follow a random thought and return briefly to the conversation when something that is said registers with you. You notice something about the speaker and go through a process of evaluating him, the way he dresses, the way he speaks. He catches your eye. You listen intently for a moment before another thought steals your attention. By the end you have accumulated just enough information to know what was being spoken about and probably just enough to avoid looking foolish if questioned. The substance of what has been said and any sub-text you will have missed completely.

Listening to reply. You are deeply involved in the conversation. It is something that interests you. You listen to what is being said and follow the flow of the conversation. Your thoughts start to hijack your listening. You know what the other party is saying. You know where they're coming from. You've got a better idea, a more informed opinion. You know what to do. You become desperate to make your point. You no longer notice what is being said. You are impatient to respond. You try to interrupt... The reality is that you have hardly heard a word of what has been said to you because you've been listening to reply.

Listening to understand. You clear down your thoughts. You concentrate on what is being said. You establish eye contact. You don't allow yourself to be distracted by stray thoughts. You don't allow any non-verbal signals to interfere with your listening. You don't judge what is being said. You sit on your differing opinions and listen to the argument, note the facts. You put aside your prejudices. Your body language is positive. You look interested. You understand.

Because you have been listening your response is more likely to be reasoned, more appropriate, which in turn will contribute to the quality of the conversation or debate. Misunderstandings are less likely.

How you respond in a conversation is also important. If you have been listening to understand, a measured, considered response is likely to add greatly to the value of what is being said.

Pause: Give yourself time to think.

Consider: Think about what you are going to say.

Respond: Respond in a logical and measured way, setting out the points you want to make clearly and unambiguously. Ask for clarification if there's a point you don't understand.

Listen: Listen to understand.

Often in a conversation it's what is *not* said that is important. If you are listening to understand you are far more likely to pick this up, to fully understand *all* aspects of what the speaker is communicating, both consciously and unconsciously.

The only way to become a skilled listener is to pay attention and to notice when you are only half listening or listening to reply and then instantly press the refresh button. Obtain a fresh focus, concentrate on what's being said, notice nuances, remember facts, engage with the speaker. Practice until it becomes *second nature*.

Questioning

Being able to question effectively is as important as being a skilled listener. Knowing how to ask the right question in the right way at the right time is a great skill, and one that takes a great deal of practice to perfect. To be an effective and emotionally intelligent leader you have to be a skilled questioner. It is the essential skill required in developing those you lead. It is the primary tool needed to connect with people, to empathise, to learn and to understand.

How good do you think you are at asking questions? Do you think about the way you ask questions – have you *ever* thought about the way you ask questions? Most of us have probably never given it a second thought. We seem to get on all right, so what's the problem? There probably isn't a problem, but it may be that you don't realise what an enormous difference it would make to your effectiveness as a leader if you improved your ability to ask questions.

Essentially there are two types of questions:

Closed questions

Open questions

Closed questions produce yes or no answers in response to questions such as: Do you? Will you? Can you? etc. They confirm, they acknowledge, they signal that a brief answer is required, perhaps an unwillingness to enter into a conversation. They save time. Closed questions are used frequently, sometimes too frequently, and can often signal impatience or a need to control.

Open questions get answers which require thought and stimulate conversation. The 'Where?' 'When ?' and 'Who?' open questions are used to obtain facts. The 'What?' 'Why?' and 'How?' questions clarify and encourage revelation, perception and creative thought. These are the questions that raise awareness and are the ones you should use when using the coaching leadership style. (Beware of using 'Why?' too often, especially on its own. It can encourage justifications and excuses when used as a response, and is a lazy way of asking 'What?' which requires you to put more thought and detail into your question.)

Much of the success you'll achieve from questioning will be in the way you phrase the question. 'Why?' for example can sound very abrupt when perhaps that's not your intention. Your tone of voice will very often determine the type of reply you receive, no matter how carefully you phrased the question. Remember to make your questions simple. Whatever you do, ask only one question at a time. Be aware of the effect your questions are having. Notice reaction, notice body language, be aware of a change in body language, listen to the tone of the response. Adjust your style accordingly.

Skilled questioners think about the conversation they are having. If they can think about it in advance, they do. Before you start, ask yourself what it is you want from the conversation, what you want to know or discover. Even as a conversation unfolds, try to follow where it is leading. Direct it with questions if you think it would be of benefit to the outcome. Follow the interest. Remember to ask open questions. Recap on what has been said if this will add clarity. Confirm your understanding if you are unsure you have understood a point correctly or if you think that by doing so it will add helpful emphasis. Use silence. Silence, carefully and thoughtfully used, can be an extremely useful tool. It gives people time think and encourages them to open up. It allows a conversation to mature, for themes to develop naturally, for facts to be revealed. After a response to your question, don't be too quick to jump in with another question. Stop yourself before you snuff out a gem.

Good questioners promote thinking and discovery, and are always conscious of the direction and flow of a conversation. They listen to understand and respond with care.

They avoid *leading* questions – those which make your own view or opinion clear, for example:

'Don't tell me you don't think it's a good idea?'

They avoid *loaded* questions – where your view or opinion is included in the question, for example:

'Don't you agree that the new sales forecast is over-optimistic?'

They use *probing* questions when appropriate. They use them sensitively and effectively.

Effective open questions will encourage a more meaningful dialogue to develop which will allow you to dig deeper and prepare the opportunity for your probing question, the one that gets to the heart of the matter. But beware. Phrase your probing question with great care.

Think ahead. If you can, disguise the probing nature of the question. Choose the words you use and make sure they are appropriate. Don't offend or cause the conversation to be curtailed or shut down.

As your skill improves, you will notice that people open up to you more. By the way they respond to you they will signal that they have confidence in you. Endorse their decision by being open yourself. Share views and opinions. Allow them in, don't shut them out.

One of the best ways to improve your questioning skills is to observe experts. Notice how they follow the conversation, the words they use, the way they phrase their questions, how they respond. Observe their expressions and their body language. Think about the techniques they use. Think about the way *you* question and start to *think* before you question. Practice until you feel your effectiveness improving, and then just keep on doing it!

Non-verbal Communication

In nearly all face-to-face communication, non-verbal communication has a far greater impact than the words we use. Our expression, our gestures, our body language, how we look, how we smile, how we react, speak silent volumes before we have even uttered a single word. This secret code is picked up and is unconsciously decoded. Instantaneously we are supplied with an emotional response to interpret and to react to, if we decide to do so. Our skill at interpreting this code will depend upon our experience, our sensitivity, how emotionally intelligent we are.

Earlier I emphasised how important empathy was as an essential emotional intelligence competency. Your ability to read and interpret non-verbal communication will very much determine how good you will be at being able to empathise effectively. Putting the other person first is the key. Being totally selfless: sensing moods, feeling tensions, reading intentions. Observing the emotional response to your questions. Noticing body language, gestures and changes in expression.

With the emphasis on the spoken word, it is not surprising that non-verbal communication is so often ignored or not accorded the recognition it deserves.

Why? Probably because its value and significance are not totally understood. Of course we notice moods and expressions, but do we really think about what they mean? Do we allow them to fully inform our emotions? If we are self-aware, sure of ourselves, confident *and* practised enough to focus our concentration on the other person, then the answer is yes, but generally, most of us think about ourselves. We are far too concerned about what the other person is thinking about *us* to notice things about *them*. Important signals are ignored, or not even seen. We rely on unreliable words as our sole source of information, and later we are surprised when things turn out to be not what they had originally seemed.

You will remember that information is only considered to be reliable when there are at least two sources. What you *hear* is one source, and what you *notice* is another. If you only pay attention to one source of information: only to what you *hear*, your information could be flawed or unreliable.

You might find it useful to remember that 'things are not always what they seem'. Use it as a prompt to alert you to sharpen your senses and 'notice'. Use it to remind you not to take things at face value, to really 'notice', and to ensure that you are not taken in by false or misleading signals. Experienced communicators are masters of disguise. There is always a code to read, but it may be encrypted, so that the impression you get is not the true one. You need to be on your guard. Remember the person with the broad smile and the cold unsmiling eyes? What was your reaction? Were you gullible? Did you only notice the smile or did you put your trust on hold and notice more?

Spotting the disingenuous is not always easy. It's perhaps easier to do on your home territory or in familiar company. Outside your own environment codes are easily masked by other factors.

Here is an example:

EXAMPLE

You have been given some quite detailed information about the character of a person you have been asked to go and meet. The source of your information is usually reliable. You arrive at the meeting having accepted what you have been told. The person works for a sister company and you assume that you will have an affinity with him, particularly after the information you have received. Even although your senses alert you to the uncomfortable atmosphere when you first meet, you ignore them. You fail to notice the irritated expression behind the beaming smile. The aggressive posture doesn't register. After it is too late to do anything about it, you realise that your information was flawed. You have starved your code breakers of essential information. They can't help you. You are on the back foot and you fail to achieve the outcome you wanted. Remember things are not always what they seem.

The secret is to always concentrate, always notice. If you have doubts either confirm them or disprove them. Ask questions. Ask more questions. Gauge reaction. Look for clues. Notice facial expressions and how they change in response to your questions. Observe posture. Aggressive posture is easy to spot. Mirror positive postures, achieve rapport. Interpret gestures, look for emphasis. Maintain eye contact. Observe eye movement in response to your questions.

Non-verbal communication is fascinating. It is like learning another language. When you become fluent your level of understanding will increase dramatically. You will also become very aware of the way you communicate non-verbally. It might come as a shock to realise how careless you are in the way you use this language. Learn to use it for your own advantage and to improve the way you communicate.

The education of your emotional wisdom through sensitive and practiced observation will enable you to break the most sophisticated codes. You will be able to interpret non-verbal messages accurately and greatly increase your ability as a communicator and an empathetic leader.

3
Motivation

> 'If people are coming to work excited... if they're making mistakes freely and fearlessly... if they're having fun... if they're concentrating on doing things, rather than preparing reports and going to meetings – then somewhere you have leaders'
> **Robert Townsend**

The downsizing which has occurred in organisations across the world has given birth to a new reality. It has altered people's focus and as a result their needs have changed.

We are all motivated by needs. In the Western world our basic need for food, water, shelter and safety are by and large secure. Our focus is now directed towards our social needs, our need to belong, for recognition, for esteem. What motivates us has changed, and how we are motivated has altered significantly too. First there was the stick. Then the carrot and the stick. This used to be an effective way of motivating people, but today they are seen as crude tools. As a carrot, money will always be a powerful motivator, but it has its limitations. It can de-motivate as easily as it can motivate, particularly when expectations are not met. On the other hand if it is used as an indication of worth and is perceived as such, it can meet a strong social need and have significant motivational value. However, what people value today is job security and a good quality of life. They want self-esteem, but self-esteem which is real and not bolstered by hollow meaningless titles, by false prestige or a large motor car. They want to be able express their potential and achieve genuine recognition for who they are and how they perform. They want to be valued and to have purpose. This posed a real dilemma in many organisations. Having made swingeing changes in their organisational structures, they found themselves ill-equipped to deliver these new needs. They desperately needed to maintain and improve performance levels, even though there were fewer people to do the job. For organisations who had a culture of leadership development, the solution was easier to find. They realised that only through effective and emotionally intelligent leadership could they meet both the new needs of their employees *and* generate the levels of individual performance that were now required. The seeds of the coaching culture were sown. People were given the opportunity – in many cases by default – to find their true potential, to identify the interferences that stood in their way, to improve their performance, to learn and to develop. There was a recognition that a breed of 'new leaders' was needed. Leaders who, in the new culture of persuasion and consent, understood that some traditional leadership methods were no longer appropriate. A *new* 'knowledge' was required. That knowledge was emotional intelligence.

'The Force'

From the beginning of time great leaders have played on our emotions in order to achieve their aims. Both by words and deeds, they motivate us by pushing our collective emotions in a positive direction. They sharpen focus and give direction. If you read some of Winston

Churchill's wartime speeches you will see exactly what I mean. He was the 'great motivator'. Through masterful verbal imagery he mobilised a nation's emotions. He gave clarity. He acted as the nation's emotional mentor. He not only increased morale, but raised levels of performance to undreamed-of heights. 'The Force' was definitely with him in those dark days.

Emotionally intelligent leaders have 'the force'. They have the power and the ability to mobilise people's emotions, to enthuse them and to motivate them. Their effectiveness depends upon their ability to understand the essential emotional intelligence competencies, to be self-aware, to know how to handle themselves, and to manage and understand relationships.

Back at the Office...

Churchillian references can seem far removed from the realities of life on the fifth floor, but if you are to motivate those you lead you need to mobilise their emotions. They too need to be enthused, they need to motivated. Remember your inspirational leadership skills? Create a vision. Paint a picture of how you see the future. Share your enthusiasm. Make sure everyone understands your long and short-term goals. Get them to 'buy-in' to them. Make them feel a part of what is going on. Let them see that you are totally committed. Don't be afraid to allow your passion to show. If your enthusiasm is genuine the motivational effect will be very strong.

Self-motivation

To motivate, *you* have to be motivated. Likely as not there is nobody looking after *your* best interests, motivating *you*, encouraging *you*. You field the frustrations of others and ensure you don't pass them on. You take the brickbats and dodge the knives.

You remain positive when things are tough. You find a way forward. You have new ideas. You have creative thoughts even in adversity. You diligently look after those you lead by being enthusiastic, by developing and motivating them. You are genuinely motivated by your work and about what the future holds. But it can get lonely. There's nobody pressing *your* adrenalin button. There are times when you could do with a bit of inspiration. Unfortunately the only person who is going to motivate you is *you*, and that can be a tough call sometimes. Self-motivation is one of the hardest things leaders have to do. This is why having a good coach can be a life-saver and can help you maintain your enthusiasm and your focus. You can also practice a version of self-coaching. This is no substitute for the real thing, but it does help you keep things in perspective and to marshal your thoughts. Here's how it works:

The purpose of **CARES** is to raise your awareness and to enable you to keep perspective.

Clear down all your thoughts. Banish all your anxieties. Start with a clean sheet of paper.

Analyse the problem which is causing you most concern.

Reframe the problem. Get a fresh perspective. What do you notice? Ask yourself what you think, what you feel. Get to the truth. Give yourself feedback..

Explore new ideas. Think of positive ways forward.

Settle on a course of action.

This process should help you to keep your thinking fresh and to avoid being swamped with matters which could severely blunt your ability to motivate others.

Praise

Praise is a great motivator. Like small children we blossom and grow when we are praised or given encouragement. It punctures self-doubt and releases enthusiasm. If there is no praise or recognition there is no joy and no motivation. Given carelessly, praise can cause resentment and confusion. Praise the wrong person and it can indicate exactly how 'out of touch' you are. To be accurate and fair is how all givers of praise should be. Praise demonstrates you notice: it shows that you care and that you are interested. If you are an observant, empathetic leader you will know the value of praise and encouragement, and use it wisely.

I don't believe that there should be set ways of giving praise, or set times when it should be given, but here are a few basic rules to remember:

- If it is expected it will have no value.
- If it is given frequently it will be meaningless.
- If it is given to the wrong person it will cause resentment.
- If it is given grudgingly it will be ignored.
- If it is buried in qualifying detail it will have little effect.
- If it is given in front of others it may be unwelcome.
- It is always wise to praise in private.
- Be even-handed. Notice if individuals go out of their way to look for praise. Notice those that steal praise from others.
- Use praise to encourage.
- Don't be predictable. Unexpected praise has a *double* value for the recipient.
- Lastly, don't forget to say 'thank you'. These two words are so often forgotten and they are very, very important. Be careless, forget this common courtesy and you will lose respect.

The Art of Criticism

We must all be allowed to learn by our mistakes if we are to develop and make progress. If you promote a forgiving culture, true learning can take place. It is therefore imperative that any criticism that is given should be constructive and positive. Criticism, no matter why it is given, must *always* have a positive purpose. Whenever possible it should be looked upon as an opportunity for improvement. Potentially de-motivating, criticism needs to be given in a manner which actually motivates the recipient to put in a better performance.

The ability of being able to deliver *good constructive criticism* is something which every leader who is committed to the development of those they lead should acquire and perfect. Here are some points to remember:

- Criticism must always take place in private, face to face.
- Never make your intention to criticise an individual known by an obvious summons in front of others, either delivered personally or by someone else.
- Never criticise in front of others.
- If you are angry about something, let your anger subside before you see the individual. Only when you are cool, calm and collected should you consider discussing the matter. Give it a lot of thought. Make sure you are clear about the outcome you want to achieve and that it will be *positive*.
- Chose the words you use carefully. Make sure the meaning is clear.
- The criticism, if it is being *given* by you must *come* from you. Don't hide behind another individual, or give the impression that the source of the criticism is from elsewhere.
- Don't attack the person's character, and never use any derogatory

words. If you do you will immediately put them on the defensive, and any hope of the meeting having a positive outcome will have lessened considerably.

- If you give the impression that the cause of the mistake was because of an unalterable flaw in the individual's character, they will cease to want to learn and stop trying. You will have planted a seed of despondency and hopelessness which will be difficult to eradicate. Please take care.
- Don't be vague with your criticism. If you want it to have the right effect, be clear about what you mean.
- In your criticism, don't concentrate only on what was not done correctly. Comment on what was done well. Give praise if it is appropriate – it will add emphasis to your criticism.
- Ask what the individual would have done differently given the opportunity again. Offer your solution if you think this will benefit the learning process.
- Use empathy. Notice the reaction to your criticism. Be sensitive to body language and facial expression. Be sensitive about the strength of your criticism. If you are too aggressive it could be counter-productive. If you are too mild it may have no impact.
- Be satisfied that genuine learning has taken place.
- Be sensitive to the fact that an individual's reaction may change having received criticism from you, whether learning took place or not. Don't single them out for special attention, but be watchful. Encouragement, thoughtfully considered and given with care, can heal and motivate.
- A successful outcome for a constructive critique should be that *both* parties should have learnt something from the process. For those giving the criticism there is much to learn from the individual's reaction to the criticism. There is perhaps something to learn

from the circumstances that caused the criticism to be made in the first place. The individual may not be suited to the task. There may be need for a reappraisal of how similar matters could be handled in future. Your knowledge of the individual will be greater, and may give you a greater insight into how you can assist their development. You should not lose the opportunity to impart some of your experience if you feel that it is appropriate and the individual concerned would benefit from it.

- The individual receiving the criticism should not leave feeling chastened or demoralised. They should feel exactly the opposite. They should feel forgiven. They should consider that they have genuinely learnt from the process. Their self-confidence should be intact, and they should be motivated by what they have learnt.

Delegation

Delegation is a very important part of the development process. If it is properly considered and well-planned, the learning which takes place can have enormous value. What delegation should *never* be is a process of getting rid of unwanted or boring tasks. Many leaders are suspicious of delegation. Misguidedly they fear the job won't be done properly, that it will erode their power, or that to organise it will take up too much time and be more bother than it's worth. It is certainly true that if delegation is to be effective it has to be well-thought-through and properly organised – and yes, it does take time. Leaders who are good at delegating are prepared to make that investment in time because they realise that there is a long-term benefit to them personally *and* to those they lead.

Intelligent delegation is a great motivator. It demonstrates a leader's faith and confidence in an individual or a team. It stimulates interest and new thinking. It can offer a new perspective and increase job satisfaction enormously. For this to happen it must be carefully considered and well planned. Here is a guide to the art of delegation:

Plan. Time spent on planning and preparation is *never* wasted. Plan exactly what you want done. Prepare as much information as you can to make the task easily understood: background, current situation, other factors which may have an effect. Be absolutely clear in your own mind what you want the outcome to be.

Select the individual for the task with care. Consider whether you should choose the individual who you think would be best suited to carry out the task, or someone who may have less experience but would benefit and learn from being given the responsibility. Weigh up the effect this may have on your time and on the outcome you want to achieve. Remember, whoever you choose, delegation is *not* an abdication of responsibility. The ultimate responsibility is *still yours*.

Allocate the task. Brief carefully and clearly. Make sure there is no ambiguity. Confirm understanding. State the outcome you are looking for. Allocate the necessary resources – *including time*. Don't cast the individual off into the unknown – make it clear what support they can have from you or from others.

Leave them alone! Resist the temptation to interfere. Keep out of the way. Let them get on with the task in hand. If you interfere there will be no learning and you will cause frustration and resentment. Also, the chances of a successful outcome being achieved will be significantly reduced.

Monitor. Monitor progress by having (agreed) progress meetings or reporting procedures – brief if possible – and which should not be seen as an interference.

If you delegate sensibly and spend time making it work, you will make your task as a leader considerably easier. It should enable you to concentrate your efforts on other things and allow you essential space for creative thought. It should also generate trust, and give greater job satisfaction to those you lead.

4

Influence

'The key to successful leadership is influence, not authority'
Kenneth Blanchard

Imagine influence as a currency. Currency has a value. Your influence as a leader depends upon the value of your currency – not on your position, your title or even your talent for showmanship. Like the currency of any sound economy it is based on real things, important things. Similarly, the value of your currency is a very accurate barometer of your success and the level of influence that you have.

The following are the main points which determine the value of your personal currency and therefore your influence:

Your competence. You must know what you're doing. You must have the ability to carry out your tasks efficiently and competently, and others must recognise the fact that you do. You should always be hungry to learn and have an enquiring mind.

Your performance. Your personal performance and the

performance of the people that you lead is the single most important factor supporting the value of your currency. If your performance deteriorates so will the value of your currency.

Your reliability. For people to have confidence they need to feel that you are reliable – that you are a safe pair of hands. That your value won't plummet overnight because you take unnecessary risks or make bad decisions

Your future. People must see that you have a future and believe in your vision. They need to believe that you have very good prospects and feel confident in investing in you.

Your judgement. You are seen to have sound judgement. People have trust in the decisions you take.

Your ability in a crisis. In a crisis you show leadership and have sound common sense. You can see a way forward in a crisis and will always work positively to reach a solution.

Your reputation. You have a sound reputation, particularly as a leader who sees the importance of empowering others by developing their skills and talents. As a result you command freely-given loyalty and support from those you lead. You have integrity.

Your ability to communicate. In the context of influence this means more than your ability to get your message across – which is of course important. It is also about empathy. Having the ability to tune into the emotions of others and achieve a better understanding and a clearer perspective as a result.

Your social awareness. You need to have a keen organisational awareness. To be astute politically and to be sensitive to relationships and social networks.

The level of influence with those to whom you report, or with those that you lead, will depend largely on your ability to maintain the value of your currency. To take the currency analogy a little further, you can suffer a serious devaluation if one of the fundamentals goes awry or your performance deteriorates. On the other hand you can grow your influence significantly if your performance increases.

Real influence has to be earned. It doesn't appear overnight. It has to be hard won. It has to be based on fact rather than fantasy. If it is not it will have little long-term value.

If the fundamentals are in place, there are things that leaders can do to strengthen and broaden their influence. Here are some of them:

Networking

If you communicate effectively you will get recognition, and recognition will lead to influence. This may be a little simplistic, but it shows that communication in its broadest sense is a vital component in achieving influence.

Networking is about communicating. It's about establishing bonds and relationships, about being known and increasing your sphere of contacts. It's having a network of contacts inside and outside your organisation on whom you can call for support, for ideas, for recommendations, for advice. For a hard-pressed, hard-working leader to spend time networking is an extremely good self-discipline. It can add a fresh perspective and supply a positive input. If you think that you have more important things to do, just remember that time spent networking is seldom wasted.

Some people find networking easy – they do it almost automatically. Others find they have to work at it and don't like to 'put themselves about', regardless of the advantages that may stem from doing so. Whatever the case it takes conscious and diligent effort if it is to be really effective. Here are some ideas which may help improve your networking skills:

- Be seen, be known, get to know. This is the first rule of networking.

- Take time with people. Go out of your way to meet people and engage them in conversation. Don't leave immediately after meetings – talk to people! Go to functions, association meetings. Get to know people outside your immediate circle.
- Keep a note of people you meet, not just their contact details, but what they do, who they know etc. Record something different about them to jog your memory.
- When you meet people, be interest*ed* and be interest*ing*. Ask questions, learn. Build your knowledge.
- Look for common ground and shared interests. Trust your instincts about people.
- If you can, pass on unsolicited information or help if you think it would be useful to the other person. The more you give the more you will receive.
- Be pro-active. Keep in contact. Find reasons to make contact. Offer invitations. Do not lose touch.
- Do not be disingenuous – it is easily spotted.
- Make the extra effort. It always pays off. Never let an opportunity to make a useful contact pass you by.

Networking should become second nature to you. If you are diligent about your networking it will be of enormous help to you throughout your career, and your influence will be enhanced as a result.

Example

Much of your influence, especially with those you lead, will depend on the example you set. As a leader you always have to be conscious that whatever you do or say will be noted by someone. Accumulated information about how you react to certain situations or to people will be used to form an impression of you as a leader. You should always be aware of this. It means that you have to sacrifice some of your freedoms. For example, the freedom to say what you want, when you want. The freedom not to be concerned about the effects of what you say or what you do. The freedom to conduct yourself in a way that does not take others into consideration. The freedom to be selfish.

It is wise to remember that example – good and bad – is contagious. Remember too that you are very likely to have many imitators, so your influence will permeate deep into your followers' psyche. This will have a very significant effect on the culture that evolves within their working environment.

I'm sure you understand how crucial the example you set is to your ability to function as an effective leader. It is your responsibility – in fact it is your *duty* – to others *and* to yourself to set the best possible example.

Here are some areas where the example you set will be especially important:

- **Integrity**. Be seen to have integrity. Be scrupulously honest about everything. If you are not, there will be no trust.

- **Performance**. If you want others to perform you have to produce results too. This does not mean that you always have to be the one who leaves the office last. This is as much about your creativity, your imagination, your flair, and your ability to inspire as it is about putting in the hours.

- **Humility**. Your success depends as much upon those who support you as it does on your own ability. Acknowledge that. Don't be afraid to ask for advice. Don't let pride get in the way.

- **Behaviour**. Remember that you are always 'on stage'. Be true to yourself and to those you lead and you won't go far wrong. How you behave to others, how you behave in a crisis, are very important. So are your manners. Rudeness, thoughtlessness, selfishness will reveal your weaknesses and devalue your influence.

Unpunctuality is selfish and sloppy. Courtesy, thoughtfulness and selflessness will enhance your influence and your ability to be effective.

Caring. The way you attend to human relations will be the hallmark of your leadership ability. Take the time to listen, to communicate, to counsel. Put others' interests before your own. Give your time freely and generously. Notice. Care. Be sensitive to situations, to emotions and to people.

Effective leaders lead by example and live by their example.

5
Teams: Leading with Emotional Intelligence

'Coming together is a beginning, staying together is progress, and working together is success'
Henry Ford

Why teams? The simple answer is greater performance. Decisions taken by a group or a team are considered to be better than those taken by an individual. Well, are they? The answer is a qualified 'yes'. The qualification? There are two. The first is if they are properly led. The second is if the team is emotionally literate: that is, everyone in the team contributes to the emotional intelligence of the team.

The success of any team will depend largely on the team leader. Competent leaders set a positive example, generate a spirit of cooperation and harmony, excitement and discovery. They set the mood and keep a hand on the tiller to gently guide the direction of the team. They understand the emotional reality of the team and the relationships within it.

To do this they employ the inspirational, bonding, democratic and coaching leadership styles – particularly the coaching style.

For a team to function effectively and perform well, it needs to be coached. This is what good team leaders do – whether they use the term coaching or not – it is what they are doing and what they are good at: establishing the emotional reality of their team. It is vital they understand how teams function.

Team Dynamics

Every team leader needs to understand the dynamics of a team to be able to manage and lead it effectively. There are four distinct stages in the development of a team. The model most commonly used is:

Forming – Storming – Norming – Performing

Forming

When we are unsure we are cautious. We keep our cards close to our chest. We don't give anything away. In a group we are anxious about fitting in, whether or not our face will fit. We are not controversial. We want to be included. We smile a lot and appear interested. We want to be liked. We want to please. Everyone appears to get on. We listen and we observe. We are highly sensitive to non-verbal communication. We play games and may not be entirely honest with each other. Everyone's focus is concentrated solely on their own emotional needs. Does this sound familiar to you?

At this stage there is a genuine desire to make the team work, for people to come together and to cooperate and to achieve results, to conform and not to rebel or be contentious. But this is also a period of unreality, a period of posturing and pretence where true feelings rarely surface.

Attention is soon turned towards the leader for confirmation of acceptance and for guidance. This is a particularly important time for leaders. They need to observe and listen carefully: to try and understand the feelings and the relationships that are developing within the team. It is also vital at the outset that they demonstrate openness and a willingness to share *their* feelings. Only when the majority of the team feels comfortable and believes that they are very much a part of the team, that they are accepted, will the team move to the next stage: storming.

Storming

In this stage confidence within the team starts to grow. Verbal and non-verbal communication has been thoroughly assimilated. Opinions have been formed about other team members. Strengths and weaknesses have been probed and noted. Individuals start to flex their muscles and try to establish a power base within the team. Disagreement surfaces and conflict looms on the horizon. Each team member tries to ensure that their opinion predominates. They try to convert others to their way of thinking. The leader stands in the firing line with the team making up the firing squad. It is crucial that the team leader answers this challenge and deals with it effectively.

At this point the team's focus is inward-looking, concentrating on internal rivalries and on each other rather than any common goal.

Norming

This is the most important stage for the team leader. This is the 'melting pot' stage, where things come to a head. Dissent surfaces. Differences that have arisen have to be reconciled through discussion and logical argument. Team members have to be prepared to give and take, to understand and even accept another team member's point of view. A good team leader will harness the energy and enthusiasm of the team and ensure that it is steered in a positive direction by encouraging members to take responsibility for their positions. They will try and divert the focus from internal division to addressing the common goals of the team. They will avoid imposing their authority no matter how tempting it might be. Challenges have to be *fielded*, not *avoided*. How a leader handles this stage of the process will very much determine how well the team performs. It requires extreme patience and the ability to coach the team so that they communicate with each other, understand other members' perspectives and acknowledge differences.

Performing

The performing stage is when the team is in 'flow', when everything comes together and the team starts to gel. Team members put aside their differences and cooperate to achieve the common goal. This does *not* mean that all is happiness and light and that there is no dissent – far from it – but it *is* a time when the team *becomes itself*. Decisions are made without fuss or rancour. The team has a clear common purpose: it has vision, clarity, and is at its most creative.

Having reached this stage it does not follow that the team will remain there forever. It is very likely that it will revert to the Forming or Storming stage again. This is not as depressing as it sounds. The more it happens the more mature the team becomes. Understanding and trust between team members is strengthened.

This process does not apply exclusively to teams. You will probably have encountered each of these stages in a totally different context. What is important to you as a leader is that you recognise them and understand them *whatever* the context.

Grasping the Reality

Teams develop their own character, their own culture. How this develops and in what form it occurs is very much down to the influence of the team leader. Once established, this culture is difficult to change, so the initial stages of team formation are always crucial to the way the team performs. Team leaders should understand the nature of their teams. They should be able to feel its pulse and be able to judge its state of health. They need to understand its reality, its emotional reality.

As an emotionally intelligent leader you are self-aware and have clear goals and an ideal vision. An emotionally intelligent team has to have a collective self-awareness. Members must understand how the team works: they must know its strengths and weaknesses, where its fault lines lie. They should be aware of the moods and emotions within the team and be sensitive to them. Just as with an individual, infectious moods and emotions can seriously affect the performance of a team. A good team leader who is in tune with the team should be able to diagnose an infection in its early stages and take the necessary steps to see that it doesn't spread.

It is the job of the leader to help the team understand and to identify the emotional reality of the team. They need to be made aware of what is happening within the team, and understand the reasons behind their feelings and emotions. The team leader is in a unique position to be able to do this: even although part of the team, the leader should preserve enough separation for there to be real objectivity. The team have to be confronted with reality and take responsibility for it. They must be made aware of what is going wrong and be given direction and guidance to rectify the situation. A team which has grasped and understood its reality, its emotional reality, will be in a position to maintain and improve its performance and move forward.

The Power of Coaching

There is no other way of putting this. To be a good team leader you need to be a good coach. At the very least you should be able to manage your team using the coaching leadership style, and to fully understand the dynamics of coaching.

Teams are a means of promoting better performance. Coaching is the most effective way of improving performance. Remember 'Potential minus Interference = Performance'? This applies to teams as much as it does to individuals. Throughout the 'Forming, Storming, Norming, Performing' process of team building, interferences come to the surface which are going to have a very negative effect on the way the team will eventually perform. The most effective way a team leader can make the team aware of, and take responsibility for, these interferences is by the use of coaching. Let's examine what some of these interferences might be in the various stages:

Forming
The interferences at this stage might be mild and are more likely to be about emotional needs and concerns rather than anything else.

- Unease
- Doubt
- Anxiety
- Reservation
- Insecurity

Storming

- More serious interferences start to surface
- Suspicion about the motives of other team members
- Intransigence
- Lack of trust

Need to dominate
Rivalries
Pursuit of hidden agendas

Norming
Dissent
Reconciliation
Acceptance of another viewpoint
The emotional reality of the team
Acceptance of common goals

Performing
This is the stage where all the interferences have been removed and the team is 'in flow' and performing at its best – where the effects of a team leader's coaching efforts will be seen to bear fruit.

Dealing with Interferences

So how would a team leader set about reducing the interferences? Above all else it's important that the team leader has a positive relationship with the team. A feeling of openness and honesty should predominate and should be a foundation for trust. The example that the team leader gives should be one that the team is happy to emulate. There should be a feeling of cooperation and inclusion, not domination or control. Here are some ways in which a team leader can reduce interferences:

Developing Ground Rules

If a set of ground rules are established and agreed upon at the outset, this will go a significant way towards reducing interference within a team. The ground rules should encompass how the team is going to operate. This should include things such as meeting schedules, support systems for team members, and suggestions from the team. The team should meet and agree the ground rules with the aim of trying to minimise interferences that might surface in the future. They should ensure that the ground rules support the aims of the team. Ground rules should *not* be set in stone, and should be reviewed *regularly*.

Highlighting Contentious Issues

It is far better that these are aired at the beginning of the life of a team rather than being allowed to fester and resurface at some later date. If team members can talk through contentious issues and can understand each other's perspective at the outset, it will lead to far greater understanding in the future.

One-to-one meetings

The more a team leader knows about each member the better. It may be that you know each member of your team well, but whether you do or don't I believe there's enormous value in having a one-to-one meeting with each team member at the outset. This will help you understand the individual much better, allow potential areas of conflict to be aired, and enable you to identify any obstacles which might affect the team's performance. This is also when the goals and purpose of the team can be set out clearly by you. It's an opportunity to bond and to discover common interests. The knowledge and understanding you acquire at this meeting will be invaluable. It will greatly enhance your ability to lead and to coach the team effectively.

Agree common goals

If a team is to make any progress it is essential to agree common goals. Goals should be established to ensure that all members of the team are pulling in the same direction. It will highlight any dissent, disagreement or confusion as to what the team's goals are. There needs to be 'collective buy-in'.

Promote active listening

'Half-listening' and 'listening to reply' flourish in a team environment. Team members can become so consumed by their own self-interest, by their need to make their point, to ensure that their opinion prevails, that they don't listen properly. They start to listen selectively. What *they* have to say becomes all-important. What *other* people say doesn't register. Misunderstandings occur and progress is severely hampered. What a well-functioning team should practice is 'listening to understand'. It is fundamentally important to the performance of the team. In the Performing stage, when the team is 'in flow' this is more likely to happen – sometimes as a matter of course because the whole team is working together and is very focused – but active listening *has* to become part of how each team member operates. Team leaders should spend time helping team members to improve their listening skills.

Coaching in Practice

As I mentioned earlier, having a one-to-one session with each team member before the team gets down to business is invaluable to a team leader. It facilitates the building of relationships and makes the whole process of leading and coaching the team so much easier and more productive. Team coaching is no different from that of coaching an individual. It's about building awareness and responsibility. The more aware and responsible the team, the better it will perform.

A lot of people ask 'Isn't team coaching more complicated – after all there are more people involved?' The honest answer is yes, it can be more complicated. The fact that there are more people involved changes the dynamics considerably. It can take longer to reach a level of clarity. There are more opinions and disagreements. Infectious doubt, when it occurs, can swamp the team and is difficult to eliminate. Consensus can be hard won. On the positive side, a team 'in flow' can achieve remarkable clarity very quickly and achieve its goals with ease.

Every team leader needs to realise that the success of any team is dependent upon three main elements:

1. The emotional reality of the team is understood.
2. The team understands and is clear about what the team task is.
3. The team knows how to achieve a successful outcome.

The role of the team leader is to facilitate this process by coaching the team so that it can achieve its objective. Let's examine how this might be done:

Developing consensus

In the development stage the emphasis is on coaching the team through the various stages – Forming, Storming, Norming, Performing – so that they are able to perform. This entails getting the team to set goals, to understand the reality. There must be a thorough examination and discussion on all the options available. A way forward must be agreed and the will of the team secured so that they will carry out what is required within an agreed time frame. The most useful coaching model to use in this instance is the INTO GROW model. (see Appendix A). Within this process there is room for a great deal of flexibility. This is a good opportunity for the team leader to encourage the team to brainstorm their ideas, to generate enthusiasm, to direct the team towards a positive way of thinking and to confront interferences. It allows the team to become more aware and responsible and therefore more able to achieve 'flow' when they reach the performance stage.

Group coaching

The secret of successful group coaching is really no different from that of individual coaching. It's about effective listening and skilful questioning using open questions: 'What?', 'Why?', 'Where?', 'How?', 'When?'. Questions to encourage, to enquire, to steer, to review. Questions to get balance within the team and to bring everyone into the discussion. A good leader and experienced coach will also know when to say nothing, to stay silent. The use of silence is a highly effective tool. In a team coaching scenario it is very often the case that the team will take things forward on their own account and there will be no need for any intervention from the team leader. There may even be signs that the team is starting to coach itself. Listen to how their questions are phrased, watch their body language. This is an indication that progress is being made and that the team is moving forward.

Sometimes it can be very effective to get team members to respond to questions in writing. This has the effect of getting them to really focus on their response. It's very easy to say something off the top of your head, or to nod in agreement, but writing it down makes people think. The team leader can then deal with the responses in different ways, through open discussion or through discussion in groups. Both can be equally effective, helping to bring both clarity and understanding. Greater commitment can follow.

Flow

I have used the term 'flow' several times and I think it deserves a fuller explanation.

Put very simply, flow is what happens when 'it all comes together'. It happens when a team reaches the performance stage, when all the interferences have been addressed, when the team understands and owns its emotional reality, when everything comes together and there is a *sense of enjoyment* within the team. Another way of putting it is that it is a mental state of effortless concentration. Pete Sampras is 'in flow' when he wins a Grand Slam. Michael Shumacher is 'in flow' when he wins a Grand Prix. I'm sure that you've experienced a time when everything just seemed to click. It could have been playing sport or it could have been at work. A time when you were hardly aware of what was going on around you, when you had no sense of time. When you were concentrating really hard, but were not aware of it. When your goals were crystal clear and nothing else mattered. Reflect on an experience you can remember like this and you will understand what I mean. 'Flow' is what happens when all your interferences have been cleared down and you are operating at the level of optimum potential. If you've been there, and I'm sure you have, I think you will agree it's an extremely enjoyable experience. Your purpose as team leader is to help your team achieve their optimum potential, to achieve 'flow'.

Top Team

Top performing teams can produce amazing results. They are able to reach 'flow' easily. These teams are no overnight phenomenon. They evolve over a period of time, having been painstakingly guided and coached by an emotionally intelligent leader, who will have encouraged their individual talents and steered them towards a higher level of performance. A lot of hard work and commitment will have been invested to establish a positive culture and develop a set of common values. In the process, relationships within the team will have matured, and interferences – particularly those of a personal nature – will have been overcome. Within the team the interactions between team members will display a high level of emotional intelligence. Empathy will be the norm. They will have learnt how to work effectively with each other. Collectively and individually, the team will be emotionally literate. This changes the role of the team leader who now no longer has to be part ringmaster, part coach. The leadership role becomes less pronounced as the team embraces a collective power. The team leader has the freedom to make a more effective contribution by working more closely *within* the team. What results is a team which is effectively able to manage itself. Everyone, not just the team leader, is responsible for keeping the team focused and operating within its ground rules. The team gains a sharper focus on its goals and there is a real clarity of purpose. It has come about through intelligent and selfless collaboration and consensus. This is not a time to sit back however: the team leader has to be diligent and remain sensitive to team behaviour. It's not always plain sailing: emotions *will* surface, differences *will* arise. An experienced leader will be able to spot these and deal with them before they are allowed to grow and become an issue – with luck without the team members noticing.

Top teams produce top results. Top teams are led by leaders who are prepared to invest in the learning and development of their teams. Top teams are emotionally intelligent teams.

The Team Leader

To be the paragon, to be constantly under the spotlight, is a very exacting experience. It is especially so for a team leader. It is a very concentrated process juggling egos, setting and monitoring the ground rules, identifying interferences, extracting commitment, generating harmony, finding 'flow' and producing results. My purpose of restating some of these points is that unless you are some sort of super human, you will need to have your batteries recharged from time to time or you will go flat and lose the plot. All the time, effort and energy you have invested in your team will start to ebb away. You will become emotionally and mentally spent. You need to have access to positive and helpful input. My recommendation is that you have regular coaching. This, I believe, will help you keep your dreams alive and enable you to explore and bring to the surface problems and pains which might interfere with your ability to be an effective team leader.

The role of the team leader is pivotal. This may seem an obvious statement, but in the relative intimacy of a team, the glare of the spotlight is twice as intense. The example and behaviour of the team leader are central to the character and performance of the team, perhaps more than in any other leadership scenario. Their effect is magnified – even for an experienced team leader. It is a walk on a tightrope, not a walk in the park. It requires concentrated effort – *all the time*. It is therefore very important that the team leader engages with the team, not just at the beginning, but every time it meets. What is also crucial is that the team leader leaves any unhelpful baggage outside the room. No disruptive or distracting mood or attitude should be allowed into the room because the first thing that has to be tackled is the moods and attitudes of others, of the team. If these are not dealt with, the performance of the team will be affected.

I have emphasised the use of coaching in bringing the team to its full potential. Coaching heightens the team's emotional awareness and helps it reach new levels of understanding and cooperation. It is by far the most effective tool the team leader has at his disposal, but, as with other leadership styles, it is even more effective when it is used in conjunction with others. In the case of a team, the styles that play the most effective supporting role to coaching are 'bonding' and 'democratic'. Bonding helps create an atmosphere where loyalty, commitment and a sense of belonging can flourish. It creates opportunities for encouragement and feedback, and provides a foundation on which trust can be built. A democratic approach encourages communication. It fosters consensus and purpose: two of the most important building blocks in the creation of a successful team.

Sensitive to the emotions and feelings of a team, an effective and emotionally intelligent leader understands the importance of establishing, together with the team, a set of ground rules. These ground rules are important to get right. If they are not, the result will be confusion and disagreement. They need to be 'owned' by the team and understood by each member. If this is the case, the team will adopt a way of operating which will allow it to optimise its potential.

Lastly, team leaders must have the courage and determination to deal with problems or issues *when they arise*. This may seem like common sense, but it is all too easy to sweep a problem under the carpet or to ignore it altogether and hope that it will go away. It won't. In a team environment problems grow and multiply very quickly. If they are not addressed promptly they are very likely to severely compromise the functioning of the team. Deal with issues. Don't avoid them.

6

All Change

*'Change is only another word for growth,
another synonym for learning.
We can all do it and enjoy it if we want to'*
Charles Handy

Change is exciting. Change is healthy. Change is reality. The speed at which change now takes place would have been unimaginable only a few years ago. Social, political and economic change has been driven by a dramatic leap in technological capability which shows no sign of slowing down. Information is common currency. As the pace of business continues to accelerate, change through necessity has become the order of the day. Side-stepping the need for change has not been possible. Maintaining the status quo is *not* an option. Comfort zones and backwaters have all but disappeared. The curtain has been firmly pulled back and there is no avoiding the penetrating beam of the spotlight. There is no hiding place. Impersonal, distant leaders, whose training and experience has centred on the more functional aspects of leadership and who have paid the emotional and personal dimension little attention, have found the new reality difficult to come to terms with. The only choice has been either to embrace change or to develop an interest in gardening.

The effect of these changes has been to significantly influence their surrounding culture. Cultures, some of them long established, have had to change, and culture change is driven by performance. Because of the speed of change, the pressure to perform has become intense. This has placed an enormous strain on leaders. Stress levels have reached new heights. It has become increasingly apparent that this new reality requires a new breed of leaders. Strong, effective and intelligent leaders who have the ability to manage their emotions, who can retain focus under extreme pressure, who can articulate vision and generate enthusiasm whilst dealing with the complexities and disruption that change can bring. The quality that is required of today's leader is emotional intelligence. This has become the era of the emotionally intelligent leader.

The Change Programme

Change comes more easily to emotionally intelligent organisations that invest in leadership development. Why? Because emotionally intelligent leaders are the conduits of successful change. They have the right mindset. They make the right connection. They understand the power of empathy. They use their leadership styles effectively and appropriately. They make change possible.

Whatever the cause for change, any change programme should be painstakingly planned and prepared before it is implemented. If it is not, disruption and discord will be the result and there may be serious long-term damage. A change programme should have the following:

Priority

Clarity

Purpose

Sustainability

Priority. Any change programme needs to be driven from the top. It must have the unqualified support and endorsement from the highest level to ensure it is given the necessary recognition and priority. This must be *seen* to be the case. If it is not it will fail. There are no half measures. Delegating the responsibility is no substitute for personal involvement.

Clarity. What are the changes? Which departments does it involve? Who does it affect? Who is involved in running the programme? What is the timetable? Select those who are going to be involved in the implementation of the changes carefully. Make sure that every aspect is covered and that every individual is clear about the programme, that they 'sign-up' to its aims and to its purpose.

Purpose. The reason for change of any sort will always be challenged. The need or the reason for change must therefore be made very clear indeed. There must be no ambiguity. In the planning process this aspect has to be given top priority. Questions that will be asked should be gone over in detail and the answers should be rehearsed. These answers should be sound and they should be honest.

Sustainability. The reason for change will be challenged, but so will the implementation and the practice. The implementation requires detailed supervision to ensure there are no incorrect interpretations or unauthorised modifications. Changes need to be monitored to ensure they are working properly. This needs to continue until the changes have been accepted and established. Changes that are well-made, for the right reasons, which are efficiently executed, will have sustainability.

Making Change Work

'Time spent in preparation and planning is never wasted' – this has never been truer when it comes to making change work. To embark on any change programme without a period of detailed preparation and planning (which includes the involvement of those at the highest level) is not recommended and would be extremely foolish. To make it work it needs total commitment. I would recommend the following course of action:

Plan

Anticipate

Rehearse

Brief

Coach

Develop

Plan. Identifying the need for change will probably already have involved a great deal of heart-searching and heartache. Once the decision to go ahead has been made, the goal of the programme needs to be to be agreed. This should be done at the most senior level. The purpose of the programme should spelled out, and should be clear and unambiguous. The detailed plan of action that follows should be prepared and agreed at every stage.

Anticipate. People who have not been able to embrace change as a process of growing and learning will find change difficult to accept, and will view it with a great deal of suspicion. To them it foretells a period of uncertainty and disruption. It is unsettling and a cause for concern. Those with something to hide, or whose performance is perhaps not what it should be, fear discovery. These reactions need to be anticipated. The effect on other departments, on suppliers, on competitors, should also be considered (if appropriate) and their reaction anticipated. Anticipated reactions should be considered carefully and the agreed responses built into the plan.

Rehearse. An essential part of any preparation is rehearsal – both individual mental rehearsal and rehearsal amongst those involved in implementing the plan. Rehearse the briefing presentation with everybody who is involved in presenting the plan. Rehearse how the plan will be presented to whom and when – timing is very important. Rehearse responses to anticipated questions and objections. Rehearse the benefits. Obtain feedback and make improvements.

Brief. *How* people are briefed and *the order* in which they are briefed about change is very, very important. Get this wrong and you will immediately build up opposition to the plan. Be sensitive to people's feelings. Include, don't exclude. Do not leave too much time between briefings – don't allow leaks and rumours to start because some are in the know and others are not.

Use the four 'E's' when briefing to ensure clarity and understanding:

Express, Explain, Expand, Example

Express the purpose, **explain** the process, **expand** the detail, give clarity with **example**.

The most important thing a briefing of this nature should achieve is 'buy-in': to win people over to the changes being proposed and for them to work together to make it happen. This requires trust. History will play a very important part in how much trust there is, but if the lessons of history have been learnt and the briefing presentation is put across with empathy and honesty, trust will have a sound foundation on which to build. Involve people in the process from the outset. Get them committed and working for a positive outcome. Determine communication channels for discussion and feedback.

Coach. After the change programme has been announced and all the briefings have been completed, a prolonged hiatus should be avoided at all costs. Although people need to take in what has been said and be given time to understand what it involves, they should not be left in limbo too long because what follows is a period when doubts and fears start to surface. Some of them will have been anticipated, others will not. Interferences may begin to undermine potential and threaten the prospect of improved performance which prompted the need for change in the first place. These interferences are best addressed promptly through coaching – which can be internally or externally sourced. Whatever the case, if it is to be implemented effectively, coaching should form part of the support for the introduction of the change programme.

Develop. Change programmes cannot be introduced and then abandoned. They need monitoring and they need to be developed. Many of you may have witnessed what happens when the consultants leave and there is no follow-up programme in place – their good work starts to unravel and people slip back into their old ways. This must not be allowed to happen.

Flexibility and adaptability should be built in. A change programme is so important to the future health of a business that it has to receive a lot of attention. Development is vital. The initial plan will not have been perfect. In the execution there will be things that will surface which will not have been anticipated. Not all the effects of the change will have been understood. The development phase should address these issues and put them right. This process of development and monitoring should continue until the change is sustained and has become a part of the new culture.

Contributing to Effective Change

The most positive way for an emotionally intelligent leader to contribute to effective change is to promote and participate in an on-going leadership development programme. The aim of this programme is to develop future leaders who can be instrumental in implementing change when the need arises. It is a programme which has factual learning and experiential learning on both an intellectual and emotional level. The programme should be one of discovery and learning, and should be endorsed at the highest level to give it strategic priority and the commitment it deserves. Organisations which support such programmes and make this element of leadership development a part of their culture are more likely to survive and prosper in the new environment of constant change. So what are some of the key elements of such a programme? Here are five key points:

Reality. A clear understanding of the emotional reality of the organisation is essential. This reality will lie somewhere in a morass of long-established habits and ground rules. It will be reflected in the behaviour and attitudes throughout the organisation and the tone will have been set by its leaders. Be aware of the reality. Know where you are starting from. This is important if you are to understand how far you are have to go and what there is to be done. If there has been a commitment to change, and the endorsement for a leadership development programme has come from the top, this is a good start.

Culture. Understand the underlying culture. How are things done? What are the values? What systems are in place? Is the prevailing attitude a positive one or a negative one? How would you define the collective practices of the organisation: re-active or pro-active? Is there a genuine commitment to a change culture within the organisation?

Relationships. Get people to participate in a process that will allow them to know more about each other. What are their dreams, their visions? What are their long- and short-term goals? How do they view the leadership development programme and what are their views on how best to implement it? Encourage people to communicate openly. An emotional commitment will foster a better understanding, relationships will improve, and cultural change will be more readily accepted as part of the programme.

Inclusion. To make change work there has to be 'buy-in'. To make a leadership development programme work there has to be 'buy-in' too. An endorsement from the top is essential, but it is also important to include the right people. This should be done with great care. These are the people who are considered to be the leaders of tomorrow. When they are selected, make sure they understand this – it will ensure 'buy-in' and commitment.

Vision. Create a collective vision for the future. Create enthusiasm and excitement about the future. Generate passion.

Towards a Better Future

Introducing, managing and sustaining change takes positive and focused leadership. Successful leaders who lead change understand their own feelings and those of others. Because of this they are able to generate support and commitment. They connect with the people they lead. The connection is intellectual and it is emotional. It is healthy and it is involved. They have authenticity. Most important of all, they share a common vision. A vision that is heartfelt, and clearly and honestly articulated. Emotionally intelligent leaders are able to deliver change positively and effectively by turning vision into action. They make effective change possible. They lead the way to a better future.

Appendix A
Coaching model

Coaching model: **INTO GROW** – mnemonic for:

INTRODUCTION – TOPIC – GOAL – REALITY – OPTIONS – WILL

Definition of Coaching

'Coaching is unlocking a person's potential to maximise their performance and to help them develop and learn in the process.'

Introduction

First 1-1 meeting Explain how coaching works.
Introduce the INTO GROW model.
Explain that the model is used in the context of raising awareness and responsibility through skilled and detailed questioning.
Set expectations and check personal chemistry.
Explain how programme works and discover what coachee wants to achieve from coaching.

Diagnostic review Coachee's current situation, ambitions, aspirations, personal values, competencies and skills.

Examine life and career to date.
Discuss an agenda for the coaching programme.
Define goals that relate to agenda.
Discuss ground rules for the coaching programme – confidentiality, honesty, openness, feedback from coach. Confirm commitment to proceed and agree coaching contract.

Pre-session Introduction Introduce the session and discuss any feedback from the previous session – if that is what the coachee wants.

Topic

Aim: To establish an understanding about what the coachee would like to talk about.

Action	Typical questions
Identify topic *Identify scale, importance, emotional significance*	'Okay, what would you like to talk to me about?' 'What subject would you like us to discuss?' 'Why is this issue important to you?'
Drill down *Confirm, understand clarify, summarise, paraphrase, reflect*	'Tell me about that?' 'I'd like to know more about that.' 'What does.....mean?' 'Tell me what you feel about it?' 'Why do you think you feel that way?' 'Are there any other aspects you want to discuss?'

Goal

Aim: To identify and agree the goal for the session.

Goals should be SMART: Specific, **M**easured, **A**greed, **R**ealistic, **T**ime-framed.

Get coachee to 'own' (take responsibility) for the goal or 'outcome'.	*I understand your topic for the session, tell me what you'd like to get out of the session?.'*
	or
Confirm, understand clarify, summarise paraphrase, reflect	*'And tell me what you want out of this session.'* *'How detailed do you expect to get?'* *'What sort of time-frame are we looking at?'*
Establish longer term vision. (Outcome)	*'What would you say would be a good outcome for this session.' (What is your goal?)* *'What would be the most helpful thing for you to take away from this session?*

Reality

Aim: To get the clearest possible understanding of the situation, to establish the 'reality'.

Objectivity: Clear down opinions, judgements, expectations, prejudices, concerns, hopes and fears that distort the perception of reality. Achieve awareness and clarity.

Unwrap the issues	*'Tell me about the situation.'* *'Can you give me more detail?'* *'So what have you done so far?'* *'So what actually happened?'* *'What is your greatest concern?'*
Confirm, understand, clarify, summarise, paraphrase, reflect	*'Who else is affected by this issue?'* *'Let me confirm my understanding...'* *'So to summarise....is that correct?'* *'Who else is involved?'*
Mine thoughts	*'What other action could you have taken?'*
Detachment *Bypass distortions* *Demand factual answers* *Tap the emotions*	*'What's getting in your way?* *'What were the factors that made you make that decision?'* *'What do you feel when...?'* *'What emotions are you aware of when...?'*

Focus on the senses
Feel, sound, sight.   *'What is the predominant feeling when...?'*

Encourage descriptive
terminology   *'What did you notice about....'*
Use What? When?
Where? Who?   *'What exactly does that mean?'*
How Much?   *'Tell me more about that?'*

Probe deeper levels
of awareness   *'How much do you think that it affected you?'*
Discover the inner   *'What do you think the real issue is?'*
filing cabinet   *'When did you become aware?'*
Plumb depths to   *'What was your reaction when...?'*
retrieve information   *'What did you sense about....?'*

Follow interest   *'In what way does this relate to the problem?'*
Follow train of   *'Tell me more about...'*
thought.   *'Tell me what else you notice?'*

Identify stress   *'Tell me how you feel physically about this?'*
Evoke awareness of stress   *'What did you notice about the way you felt.'*
Uncover mental attitudes
such as perfectionism

Identify inner obstacles   *'What is preventing you from...'*
- 'interferences'
Focus self-awareness   *'What obstacles do you have to overcome to...'*
on thoughts and attitudes   *'In what ways do you inhibit your potential?'*

Acknowledge their   *'What personal resistance do you have to...?'*
existence   *'What do you think are the reasons for you acting/*
       thinking that way?'

Reality questions   *'What is the real issue here?'*
Focused questions to
get coachee to think,   *'What is the bottom line?'*
to feel, to be engaged   *'What is your next step?'*

*Encourage answers to be
descriptive not judgemental*   '*What action have you taken on this so far?*'

*Question to encourage
action followed by:*   '*What were the effects of that action?*'

Options

Aim: To create a list of as many alternative courses of action as possible.

Get creative juices flowing
Encourage productive assumptions

'*So how do you want to approach the issue?*'
'*What are all the alternatives available to you?*'
What else?'

Blend ideas
Recognise benefits and cost of options

'*Where are the greatest benefits?*
'*What else?*'

Discover creative possibilities

'*What other ideas have you got?*'

Maximise choices

'*What else could you do?*'

Make list

'*What about making a list of all the alternatives?*'
'*What would you do if you could start again with a clean sheet of paper?*'

Map out the options

'*What are the advantages and disadvantages of each of these options?*'
'*Which do you think is the best option?*'
'*Which would give you the most satisfaction?*'
'*What other options are there?*'
'*What else have you considered?*'
'*Anything else?*'

Will

Aim: Achieve a specific commitment to take action within an agreed time

Commitment
Check commitment to
course of action
Coachee to 'own'
action plan

'Which of the options have you decided to choose?'

'What are the reasons for your choice?'
'How well does your choice meet your objective?'
'What's going to stop you achieving your objective?'

Measurement
'What are going to be your measures of success?'

Time
'When are you going to start?'
'How long do you expect it to take?'
'So it will be completed by....?'

Obstacles
'What obstacles might you meet along the way?'
'What action do you need to take to overcome these?'

Support
'What support do you need?'
'What other considerations do you have?'

'Will' check
'Rate on a scale of one to ten your commitment to carry out the actions you've agreed to.'
'What would you need to do to make that a ten?'

Conclusion

After the session, the coach may give the coachee an accurate written record of the action steps agreed and perhaps a summary of the answers given to the follow-up questions.

Appendix B
Goal planner

Goal
   My goal is to:

Benefits
The benefits of achieving my goal are:
1.
2
3.
4.
5.

Factors
Factors I need to consider if I am to achieve my goal are:

Factors for: Factors against:
1.   1.
2.   2.
3.   3.
4.   4.
5.   5.

Action
I need to take the following action if I am to achieve my goal:

Action: To be achieved by:

1.

2.

3.

4.

5.

Indicators
Indicators that I am making progress in achieving my goal might be:

1.

2.

3.

4.

5.

Time Plan
My time plan is:

Completion
I will have achieved my goal by:

Appendix C
Goal report

Achievement

I achieved / did not achieve my goal:

Results

The benefits have been: The consequences have been:

1.
2.
3.
4.
5.

Learning
I have learnt the following:

1.
2.
3.
4.
5.

Action
I need to take action on the following points:

Action point: To be actioned by:

1.
2.
3.
4.
5.

New Goal
My new goal is:

References

Adair, John; *Effective Leadership*, Pan Macmillan, 1993

Bennis, Warren; *On Becoming a Leader*, Arrow Books, 1998

Csikszentmihalyi, Mihaly; *Good Business*, Hodder & Stoughton, 2003

Downey, Myles; *Effective Coaching*, Texere Publishing, 2001

Gallwey, Timothy; *The Inner Game of Tennis*, Jonathan Cape, 1975

Goleman, Daniel; *Emotional Intelligence*, Bloomsbury Publishing, 1996

Goleman, Daniel; *The New Leaders*, Little, Brown, 2002

Handy, Charles; *The Age of Unreason*, Arrow Books, 1995

Mant, Alistair; *Intelligent Leadership*, Allen & Unwin, 1997

Maxwell, John; *Developing the Leader Within You*, Nelson, 1993

West, Lucy / Milan, Mike; *The Reflecting Glass*, Palgrave, 2001

Whitmore, Sir John; *Coaching for Performance*, Nicholas Brealey, 1996

About the Author

Michael Massey spent eight years in the Army, where he saw active service in the Far East, served in Germany and worked for the Defence Intelligence Staff in Whitehall. In the business career which followed, he started two manufacturing companies and built them into multi-million pound businesses.

He is founder of Michael Massey EQ Leadership Solutions, an organisation offering Emotional Intelligence leadership training, development and coaching for organisations and senior executives.

When he is not involved in lecturing or holding forums and workshops, he enjoys writing, running and flying helicopters. He is married with two daughters.

www.michaelmassey.co.uk